New Perspectives on the Vietnam War

Our Allies' Views

Edited by
William Schoenl

University Press of America,® Inc.
Lanham · New York · Oxford

4720 Boston Way
Lanham, Maryland 20706
UPA Acquisitions Department (301) 459-3366

12 Hid's Copse Rd.
Cumnor Hill, Oxford OX2 9JJ

Printed in the United States of America
British Library Cataloging in Publication Information Available

ISBN 0-7618-2382-4 (paperback : alk. ppr.)

™ The paper used in this publication meets the minimum requirements of American National Standard for Information Sciences—Permanence of Paper for Printed Library Materials, ANSI Z39.48—1984

To undergraduate students

Contents

Preface

In the autumn, salmon lie on the redds;
some politicians lie on the hustings.

This book provides new perspectives on the Vietnam War. I have strongly focused on our SEATO allies to get beyond the ethnocentrism of "U.S. views" and the amorphousness of "international perspectives." With the exception of South Korea (included in Chapter I), only Southeast Asia Treaty Organization allies—the Philippines, Thailand, Australia, and New Zealand—sent troops to support the U.S. in the Vietnam War. Great Britain, a SEATO ally, adopted a middle-ground position that supported the U.S. diplomatically but refused to send troops. Pakistan and France—the remaining SEATO allies—opposed the War.

The works I have selected are the most important and interesting that I have found from the past seven years. I have edited them to present a continuous story of the Vietnam War from the escalation of the Johnson years to the gradual withdrawal of the Nixon-Ford years. My purpose is to provide a provocative work based on multiple perspectives to get undergraduates *thinking* about the War.

I. Asian Allies:

A. Korean, Filipino, and Thai Troops

South Korea, the Philippines and Thailand sent troops to the Vietnam War. Suspicions arose and charges were made that the U.S. paid them to send soldiers, but determination of the facts had to await the declassification of documents. Robert Blackburn, who had fought alongside South Korean marines during two years of duty in Vietnam, examined declassified documents. His *Mercenaries and Lyndon Johnson's "More*

Flags" (1994)—now out of print—shows how the Johnson Administration paid for involvement of Korean, Filipino, and Thai soldiers in the War.

B. Pakistani Opposition

Why did Pakistan oppose the Vietnam War? "Reaping the Whirlwind, 1963–1965," the last chapter of Robert McMahon's *Cold War on the Periphery: The United States, India, and Pakistan* (1994), provides answers. In particular, the long-standing hostility between India and Pakistan led Pakistan to seek improved relations with China. This persistent animosity has remained to the present. Now that Pakistan and India have nuclear weapons it may take on additional significance.

II. European SEATO Allies: British Diplomatic Support, French Opposition

Caroline Page provides perspectives of major allies Great Britain and France on the Vietnam War. Yet readers unfamiliar with her *U.S. Official Propaganda during the Vietnam War, 1965–1973: The Limits of Persuasion* (1996) would not guess its European contents from the title or subtitle. In particular, her examination of British and French perspectives deserves to be read by students of the Vietnam War. She examines the interaction of U.S. official propaganda with British and French opinion—governmental and public!

III. SEATO Allies "Down Under": Australian Gradual Withdrawal

By 1968–1969—beyond Indochina—tensions in Southeast Asia were easing. Regional noncommunist governments were becoming economically and politically stronger than they had been during the early and mid-1960s. With the rift between China and the Soviet Union growing, the new Nixon Administration might attempt to play these two powers off against each other. In June 1969 Nixon began "Vietnamization" of the War accompanied by the gradual withdrawal of American troops. Not until summer 1971, however, did Australia (and its smaller neighbor New Zealand) decide on full withdrawal of their troops. Peter

Edwards' *Nation at War* (1997) depicts how the Vietnam War's continuation to 1975 affected Australian politics, society, and diplomacy.

IV. Epilogue: The 20th and 25th Anniversaries of the Fall of Saigon

To mark the 20th anniversary of the Vietnam War's end and Vietnam's entry into ASEAN (Association of Southeast Asian Nations), *The Bangkok Post* published a series of articles in 1995, initiated by an editorial. The most interesting and significant articles appeared in its weekly "Inside Indochina" section on May 2: "Quest to Rebuild Mutual Trust" and "Report" by Bhanravee Tansubhapol and Nussara Sawatsawang. With part of the editorial they are reprinted here in their entirety. Included also is an update on Vietnam from *The Bangkok Post*, April 27, 2000, by Alexander Casella, initially Executive Secretary, Asian Documentation Center, Graduate Institute of International Studies, Geneva, and later Director for Asia for the United Nations High Commissioner for Refugees.

I am most grateful to the undergraduate students in my seminars on new perspectives on the Vietnam War. Without their interest and the stimulus of many discussions this book would never have developed. Some are sons and daughters of Vietnam veterans. Some have fathers who have suffered from post-traumatic stress disorder—a disorder undefined by the American Psychiatric Association until 1980. Students want to know about the Vietnam War years before they recede more fully into the past.

I am very grateful to Lorian Wyzinski, Aaron Payne, Beth Springsteen, and Everett Vandagriff, my fine research assistants, who helped bring this book to completion. As undergraduate students themselves they helped me select material of importance and interest to students. We have added subheadings in both the Contents and the text to highlight themes. We have included discussion questions at the end of each chapter for possible use by teachers and students. We hope that they stimulate further thought and questions.

I am thankful to four professional colleagues in particular. Dr. Chalong Soontranovich, professor of modern Thai history, Chulalongkorn University, Bangkok, Thailand, suggested articles in *The Bangkok Post*. Professors Richard Laurence, a historian of peace and war, and James

Seaton, a literary critic of post-modernist thought, Michigan State University, nourished my interests in peace and justice through our conversations over many years. Professor Michael Lewis, Director, Asian Studies Center, Michigan State University, read the outline of the manuscript and made useful comments. Of course, I am solely responsible for editing this work.

It may be appropriate for courses in History and in Asian, Commonwealth, or Peace & Conflict Studies.

William Schoenl
October 2001

Acknowledgments

I gratefully acknowledge permission to reprint:

Robert M. Blackburn, *Mercenaries and Lyndon Johnson's "More Flags": The Hiring of Korean, Filipino and Thai Soldiers in the Vietnam War* (Jefferson, North Carolina and London: McFarland, 1994), pp. 1–5, 7–8, 11, 22–23, 30–32, 48–50, 52–55, 58–59, 61–65, 72–73, 80, 82–84, 88–93, 95, 98–100, 102–115. Reprinted by permission of Robert M. Blackburn.

Robert J. McMahon, *The Cold War on the Periphery: The United States, India, and Pakistan* (New York: Columbia University Press, 1994), pp. 307–308, 318–329, 331–332, 334–335.© Columbia University Press. Reprinted with the permission of the publisher.

Caroline Page, *U.S. Official Propaganda during the Vietnam War, 1965–1973: The Limits of Persuasion* (London and New York: Leicester University Press, 1996), pp. 106–110, 112–113, 120–124, 128–133, 135–144, 146–147, 149–150, 154–155, 158–159, 161–162, 165, 174–179. © Caroline Page and The Continuum International Publishing Group. Reprinted with the permission of the publisher.

Peter Edwards, *A Nation at War: Australian Politics, Society and Diplomacy during the Vietnam War, 1965–1975* (St. Leonards, Australia: Allen & Unwin in association with the Australian War Memorial, 1997), pp. 185–195, 198, 201–205, 240–241, 243–246, 262–264, 292, 297, 303–306, 313–318, 321–326, 328–329, 331–332, 335–340, 342–344. Reprinted with the permission of the Australian War Memorial. This book is from the Australian War Memorial's series, "The Official History of Australia's Involvement in Southeast Asian Conflicts 1948–1975."

The Bangkok Post: Editorial, "Southeast Asia Joins Hands in the Aftermath of a War," April 28, 1995, p. 4; Nussara Sawatsawang and Bhanravee Tansubhapol, "Quest to Rebuild Mutual Trust," May 2, 1995, Inside Indochina section, p. 1; Bhanravee Tansubhapol and Nussara Sawatsawang, "Report," May 2, 1995, Inside Indochina section, p. 2. Reprinted by permission of *The Bangkok Post*.

Alexander Casella, "Saigon: After the Fall," *Bangkok Post*, April 27, 2000, p. 12. Reprinted by permission of Alexander Casella.

Part One
The Johnson Years: Escalation

I. Asian Allies

A. South Korean, Filipino and Thai Troops

*Robert Blackburn**

Background

The official U.S. State Department title for the American program of obtaining allied aid for South Vietnam was "The Free World Assistance Program." "More Flags" is, nevertheless, the label most often attached to the program. Occasionally, the program is cited as the "Other Flags" or "Many Flags" program.

As presented to the American public in the spring of 1964, the sole purpose of the "More Flags" program of President Lyndon Johnson was to obtain free world aid for the beleaguered nation of South Vietnam. Johnson's use of the program to pursue this publicly stated goal allowed him, however, the opportunity to achieve a more important, and more covert, objective. To Lyndon Johnson, the primary purpose of the More Flags program, when first inaugurated, was to serve as a visible symbol of free world support for his Vietnam policies. Notably, when first conceived, the hiring of mercenaries to fight in South Vietnam was not one of the More Flags program's original goals.

The program's original objective to pursue only non-combat related aid for South Vietnam did not, however, survive even the first year of its existence. Even before Johnson sent American ground combat troops into South Vietnam in March 1965, less than a year after the More Flags program's inception, the program's purposes had already been redefined to allow for the procurement of free world troops to fight, and die, in Southeast Asia. . . .

Upon ascending to the presidency after John F. Kennedy's assassination [in November 1963], Lyndon Johnson brought to the office not only a finely tuned political acumen, but also a long and impressive list of legislative skills. During the many years he served in both the House of Representatives and Senate, Johnson may well have become "the most accomplished legislative strategist in American history." When John F. Kennedy was assassinated, very probably no man in the United States was better prepared than Lyndon Johnson to exercise the purely political and governmental duties that are integral to the administration of the presidency. Yet these skills, great as they may have been, ultimately proved both inadequate and flawed when applied to the defining foreign policy problem of his administration, Vietnam. . . .

Even with the French withdrawal from Southeast Asia [Indochina] after 1954, Johnson's position as Senate Majority Leader obliged him to further develop his knowledge of the region. As the Democratic leader in the Senate, Johnson was constantly involved in the development and implementation of the Eisenhower Administration's efforts to establish and support the newly formed Republic of Vietnam [South Vietnam].

In addition to his involvement with the events of the region during his tenure in the Senate, Johnson also learned more about Southeast Asian problems when he visited Saigon in 1961 as Kennedy's vice president. . . .

. . . In a private discussion with [South Vietnamese President Ngo Dinh] Diem during this visit, Johnson discreetly suggested that, if Diem were to make a personal request of President Kennedy, the U.S. would seriously consider sending American combat forces to South Vietnam. While nothing immediately came of Johnson's suggestion—Diem pointedly "displayed no interest" in pursuing the idea—the fact it was made is important. At the very least, his suggestion to Diem demonstrates that Johnson, as early as 1961, accepted the possibility that American combat troops would serve in Vietnam, a possibility that would become reality in 1965. . .

An indicator of both Kennedy and Johnson's dated foreign policy beliefs can be seen in the fact that both men maintained an absolute belief in the validity of the "domino theory" of communist conquest. This theory, accepted as official American foreign policy dogma in

1950, maintained that all Southeast Asia would fall to the communists like a row of dominoes if South Vietnam fell. It should be noted, however, that Kennedy and Johnson were not alone in their conviction that the domino theory was a realistic predictor of events. The theory also constituted a policy absolute for many senior statesmen in both presidents' administrations, a list that included both Secretary of State [Dean] Rusk and Secretary of Defense [Robert] McNamara. In a joint report to President Kennedy in 1961, the two cabinet officers forcefully assured him that if he allowed South Vietnam to fall, it would be "a near certainty that the remainder of Southeast Asia and Indonesia would move to a complete accommodation with communism, if not formal incorporation with the communist bloc." Further, after Lyndon Johnson assumed the presidency, McNamara made sure the new president received the same appraisal of the perceived danger: "Unless we can achieve this objective (prevent the fall of South Vietnam) . . . almost all of Southeast Asia will fall under Communist dominance." . . .

The birth of the More Flags foreign policy of the United States occurred at a presidential news conference on 23 April 1964. Lyndon Johnson, in response to a question about the content of possible future American assistance to the Saigon government, acknowledged that while he "anticipated" that the United States would send more aid, he hoped

> we would see some other flags in there, other nations as a result of the SEATO [Southeast Asia Treaty Organization] meeting, and other conferences we have had, and that we could all unite in an attempt to stop the spread of communism in that area of the world, and the attempt to destroy freedom. . . .

By 11 December 1964, the State Department could only report to the president that a scant 15 of America's worldwide friends and allies were then sending assistance to South Vietnam, and of these 15, only six were offering significant help (South Korea, Australia, New Zealand, the Philippines, Thailand, and Nationalist China). As for the possible participation of the rest of the free world nations, the State Department summarily dismissed the possibility of their future participation with one succinct sentence: "The actual and anticipated contributions from other countries doesn't amount to very much." The More Flags program was obviously not coming close to achieving the expectations Lyndon Johnson had of it. If the program were to succeed, something more would have to be done. More Flags had to change.

The first intimations of a modification in the More Flags program's originally stated goals came in a 3 December 1964 cable from President Johnson to Henry Cabot Lodge, America's ambassador to South Vietnam. Johnson, in a sentence added to the last page of this message, hinted at what the future would hold as far as the basic intent, purpose, and character of the More Flags program were concerned: "We propose to seek the *military* (emphasis added) and political cooperation of the governments of Thailand, the Philippines, Australia, New Zealand, and the United Kingdom."

Further evidence that President Johnson contemplated making changes of a military nature in the More Flags program is also found in letters drafted by White House officials for Johnson's signature. Each of these letters, addressed to the heads of government of Australia, New Zealand, and the Philippines, three of America's Southeast Asia Treaty Organization (SEATO) allies, contained a Johnson appeal for each leader to increase his country's aid commitments to South Vietnam. In two of these letters however, to Australian Prime Minister Robert Menzies and President Diosdado Macapagal of the Philippines, the appeal for additional aid also included a specific request for a military commitment. Of the three leaders, Prime Minister K.J. Holyoake of New Zealand alone was asked only to increase the level of his country's nonmilitary aid. While the More Flags program's original purpose, to seek nonmilitary aid for Vietnam, would continue as a component of the program throughout the remaining years of the Johnson presidency, after December 1964 this humanitarian purpose would never again be the primary goal of the program. After this date, noncombat aid fell behind military related aid, and later, combat troops, in Johnson's rank ordering of importance for the More Flags program. . . .

The failure of the More Flags program in obtaining aid from as many free world countries as possible became something of a moot point, however, after 9 March 1965. With the introduction of American combat forces into Vietnam, the primary focus of the program shifted from a simple solicitation of aid to one concentrating on recruiting troops. From the moment the first Marines waded ashore at Da Nang, the More Flags program became the mechanism through which the United States would make "an energetic effort to recruit other nations to fight with the U.S. forces in Vietnam." After 9 March 1965, the More Flags program and Lyndon Johnson's pursuit of mercenary troops to fight in support of American foreign policy goals became irrevocably linked. . . .

The Republic of Korea Commitment

The largest contingent of free world troops, approximately 50,000 men at its height, sent to fight with and for the United States in South Vietnam came from the Republic of Korea (ROK). Because of the large size of their commitment and the conditions of their service, of the five free world troop-contributing nations [South Korea, the Philippines, Thailand, Australia, and New Zealand], these Korean units became the troops most frequently accused of being American mercenaries, of being "Seoul's hired guns."

Charges that the Korean combat troops were serving in South Vietnam as a mercenary force, and not simply as South Korea's answer to a Vietnamese request for assistance, began to surface almost as soon as the first ROK troops landed in South Vietnam. These mercenary charges came, however, from critics who had little more than ideological and emotional arguments to support their allegations. Confirmation that the ROK units, and certain other allied troop units that followed them into Vietnam, were actually U.S.-paid mercenaries, could only come with the declassification of official United States government documents from the period. With the current availability of these declassified documents, it is now possible to prove that the Republic of Korea furnished the United States with mercenary troops to fight in South Vietnam. . . .

American officials, from the very start of the discussions [with the Republic of Korea], found themselves negotiating from a severely weakened position, as everyone involved in the process knew how much President Johnson wanted a ROK combat division committed to Vietnam. As a direct consequence of the Koreans having this knowledge, it was the Koreans, not the Americans, who set the negotiations' agenda. In their opening proposals in the discussions, Korean officials submitted a substantial, and to the State Department, totally unreasonable, ten item "wish-list" dealing with four general concerns: (1) Korea's need for a firm recommitment of all U.S.-Korea treaty and military obligations, (2) financial benefits accruing from a rescinding of all present and future MAP [Mutual Assistance Program] transfers, (3) the need to modernize the entire ROK armed forces, and (4) U.S. financial assistance for the entire Korean domestic economy. From the moment the Koreans introduced their "wish-list," its items became the principal points of discussion in the negotiations. . . .

After only two months of negotiations, the United States agreed, as payment for the deployment of an ROK combat division to South Vietnam, to the following:

1. There would be no United States or ROK military force reductions in Korea without prior consultation with the Korean government.
2. Concrete assurances would be given to Korea that the American defense of Korea would not be affected by any present or future American actions in Vietnam.
3. MAP funds would be increased for Fiscal Year (FY) 1966 by $7 million, with that amount to be used to fully equip three ready reserve infantry divisions in Korea.
4. The FY 1966 and 1967 MAP transfers would be suspended.
5. All ROK forces in Korea would be modernized in fire power, mobility, and communications.
6. The United States would procure as much military related supplies as possible, materiel needed in either Korea or Vietnam, from South Korean suppliers.
7. Korean civilians would be hired, whenever possible, to work in Vietnam, principally in construction projects.
8. The United States would provide all subsistence, equipment, training, logistical support, construction, and transportation for all ROK troops in Vietnam. . . .
9. Per diem overseas allowances would continue to be paid at established rates to all ROK military personnel in Vietnam.
10. American exports of foodstuffs to Korea would increase with the increase to be offered at reasonable costs.
11. The United States would provide $150 million in development loan funds to be used for projects inside South Korea in addition to whatever funds would be required at a future date for mutually agreed on development projects.
12. U.S. support for economic development projects would continue at a scale equal to or exceeding the level of current financial support.
13. The United States would provide employment and welfare relief for needy people in Korea.
14. The United States' technical assistance and training grants to Korea would continue, at present levels or higher. . . .

When Lyndon Johnson began deploying U.S. combat forces to Vietnam on 8 March 1965, he knew, if he were to maintain the image that the United States was not acting unilaterally there, that this move required other free world nations to also commit troops. It quickly became evident, however, that the majority of America's allies did not think that Lyndon Johnson's problems in South Vietnam warranted their becoming militarily involved. Only Australia and New Zealand, of all America's allies, chose to voluntarily commit their troops to Vietnam. Johnson had to do something if he was to continue representing to the American people that his policies had international support. The purchase of mercenary troops, starting with the South Korean Tiger Division, allowed Johnson to do this.

America's purchase of South Korean troops did not take into account the desires of the South Vietnamese government, on whose part the United States ostensibly obtained these troops. In its obsession with maintaining the facade of international support, the Johnson Administration spent little time worrying whether Vietnamese interests were coincidental with their own. As a consequence to these feelings, the U.S. government did not even think to include South Vietnamese government officials in the U.S.-Korean negotiations over the deployment of the ROK division to their country. Saigon's exclusion from the discussions was deemed necessary by the U.S. State Department. After all, Washington officials well knew that the Saigon government was opposed to additional Korean troops being sent to their country: "the Vietnamese show no desire for additional Asian forces since it affronts their sense of pride.". . .

. . . While it was all but impossible for Saigon to reject these ROK troops, Vietnamese government officials nevertheless managed to indicate their lack of enthusiasm for the Korean troop deployment in perhaps the only way they could. Saigon postponed making a formal request for the ROK division as long as possible, delaying until 21 June 1965 before sending Seoul a request for their troops. A cursory examination of the record will thus show that the Saigon government did formally request ROK troops; the facts behind that request, however, belie both U.S. and Korean assertions that Korea sent its troops only because Vietnam sincerely wanted them and actively pursued them.

With the deployment of the 20,000-man ROK Tiger Division, South Korea became the largest free world contributor of combat troops, save for the United States, in South Vietnam. Still, this one division was not enough to satisfy Johnson Administration needs. With the planned massive increase in the U.S. troop commitments to South Vietnam in 1966—more American combat troops, over 200,000, were sent to Vietnam in 1966 than in any other single year of the war—Washington's search for foreign troops to fight there became even more frenetic. The

Tiger division had not even completed its arrival in Vietnam when Washington notified Seoul that "additional forces [would be] required in 1966." By the time the last Tiger Division contingents came ashore in Vietnam, on 16 April 1966, negotiations for the commitment of a second ROK division had already begun in earnest. . . .

Lyndon Johnson, after the completion of his February 6–8 meeting in Honolulu with then Vietnamese Premier Nguyen Cao Ky, had ostensibly assigned [Vice President Hubert] Humphrey the responsibility of briefing America's Pacific allies on the decisions arrived at in Honolulu. At least this was the reason Johnson released to the American public. L.B.J. had, however, given his vice president other, more covert, instructions. Humphrey was instructed to use his travels to obtain more allied combat troops for South Vietnam, whatever the cost. Humphrey therefore, on his arrival in Seoul in late February, was able to assure the Koreans that, if they sent a second division to Vietnam, both the Korean government and the troops themselves would receive very favorable concessions from the United States. With Humphrey's timely intercession, the negotiations were able to get moving again.

The very fact that the Johnson Administration deemed it necessary to have the Vice President of the United States relay these assurances signaled a recognition that a fundamental change had taken place in the negotiations. In all prior negotiations, both the United States and Korea recognized that the central issue involved was Korea's diplomatic and military relationship with the United States. To this end, in the early negotiations, American concessions that strengthened Korea's ties with the United States took priority over all else. The economic aspect of these concessions, though important and not to be depreciated, nevertheless remained a secondary concern. By the beginning of the negotiations for the second ROK division, however, the rank ordering of these two concerns had switched. Korean officials now considered accrued economic benefits as the most important determinant of whether South Korea would send more of its soldiers to South Vietnam. It thus fell to Vice President Humphrey to assure these officials that all ROK troops serving in Vietnam, either now or in the future, would receive fair, just, and proper compensation from the United States government. . . .

The increased numbers of Korean troops directly engaged in combat in South Vietnam, coupled with the concomitant increase in American financial costs, still did not satiate Lyndon Johnson's desire for even more troops. The political debates within South Korea against further troop deployments, however, had become so intense by late 1966 that

President Park [Chung Hee] was forced to concede the virtual impossibility of any further ROK troop commitment to Vietnam in the near future. Thus, when President Johnson sent, in August 1967, his blue-ribbon presidential mission of Maxwell Taylor and Clark Clifford to Seoul to solicit even more Korean troops, they came away empty-handed. That the Koreans would reject the entreaties of the Taylor-Clifford mission was not unexpected, as the Koreans had already rejected requests from President Johnson during his state visit to South Korea in November 1966, and from South Vietnam's Premier Nguyen Kao Ky when he visited Seoul in January 1967. . . .

. . . Though President Park himself continued his personal support of all American requests for more ROK troops for South Vietnam, his support alone no longer guaranteed Korean National Assembly support. In the December [1967] meeting, Park admitted that with the current strength of his political opposition in the National Assembly, there was little chance he could now muster the support to deploy further ROK troops to Vietnam. . . .

. . . Despite [U.S.] Ambassador [to Korea William] Porter's continuing best efforts, and in spite of an almost constant flow of Johnson Administration petitions to President Park and the South Korean government for additional troops for Vietnam, events which neither Washington nor Seoul could control would soon occur that guaranteed that Seoul would send no further troops to aid the Saigon government. Two events of January 1968—President Park's narrow avoidance of assassination by a North Korean death squad and the North Korean capture of the U.S. spy ship *Pueblo*—successfully cast the new South Korean policy in stone. Playing up the idea that the "deployment of both U.S. and South Korean resources to Viet Nam might have helped to provoke the incidents," President Park's opposition now managed to garner enough votes in the National Assembly to prevent any further ROK involvement in Vietnam. And no amount of American assurances could convince them to change their minds. After January 1968, the Korean National Assembly considered no Washington plea for more Korean troops. . . .

Even if Korean security had not become the National Assembly's uppermost concern by 1968, the situation was such by then that the United States could no longer reasonably expect to obtain further Korean troops, no matter how generously they paid them. The fact was that by 1968, the principle factor militating against the United States' obtaining more troops was not the threat posed by North Korea, but the vast amount of American economic aid the Koreans were already receiving for the ROK troops then in South Vietnam. Simply stated, because of the large amounts of American aid already flowing into South Korea, the national economy was saturated and thus could not appreciably benefit from an infusion of more aid. Consequently, many Korean officials thus believed that further ROK troop deployments to Vietnam were not only economically unnecessary but potentially detrimental to the economic well-being of Korea. . . .

Clearly, the United States paid very substantial sums to the Republic of Korea for the use of their military forces in South Vietnam, a largess which also directly benefited the individual Korean soldier. From the moment that a Korean soldier set foot on Vietnamese soil . . . he started to draw pay substantially higher than he would have had he not elected to serve there. A Korean private, earning a base salary of $1.60 a month, could earn almost that much, from $1 to $1.25, with one day's service in Vietnam. Nevertheless, even though the individual Korean soldier received a financial bonanza for his service, the cost of his service to the United States still constituted a bargain. By buying the services of a ROK soldier, the United States only had to pay out between $5,000 and $7,800 a year, while it cost the U.S. government about $13,000 a year to support an American soldier in Vietnam.

The Philippines Contingent

Not surprisingly, [Philippine President] Macapagal's justifications [for sending aid to Vietnam] were predictably self-serving, presenting only the most beneficent motives for his administration's actions. To Macapagal, the Philippine nation, government, and people were sending aid to Vietnam only because of their deep and abiding commitment to democracy and freedom. And if this justification alone proved insufficient, Macapagal cited the Philippine government's obligations as a member of the Southeast Asia Treaty Organization (SEATO) as an added reason for their sending aid to Vietnam. This latter rationale was, however, not original with Macapagal, as he borrowed it from the United States. According to American reasoning, and the Philippines mimicked the position, the United States was obligated to aid Vietnam because of its SEATO treaty obligations. The use of this argument was especially appealing to the political leaders of the two countries because with it their actions gained some semblance of international validation.

The use by either the United States or the Philippines of SEATO obligations to justify their actions in South Vietnam, however, was spurious. Although the two countries were SEATO members, South Vietnam was not. Therefore, there existed no *pro forma* obligation for any SEATO member to act in defense of any threat to Vietnamese national sovereignty. Even further, SEATO, as an organizational unit, never adopted an official policy position for or against its members becoming involved in Vietnamese affairs. A major reason why SEATO chose not to get officially involved was the opposition by two SEATO members, France and Pakistan, to any SEATO action in Vietnam. As a direct consequence of French and Pakistani antipathy, the United States actively worked to prevent any question of South Vietnamese aid from being addressed in any formal SEATO organizational meeting. The United States, however, and by extension, the Philippines, never permitted the true state of affairs to interfere with their continuing to use SEATO obligations to justify their actions in South Vietnam during the remainder of their involvements in the Vietnam War. . . .

. . . On 19 February 1965, Secretary Rusk notified the embassy in Manila to inform the Philippine government that the United States would agree to their deploying a 2,300-man engineering task force to South Vietnam at a funding level of $9.13 million a year. While Secretary Rusk's acceptance of the $9.13 million figure indicated his tacit acceptance of many, but not all, of the Filipinos' demands, the message also made it clear that Secretary Rusk had not made these concessions with equanimity. In a forceful caution to the American negotiators in Manila, Secretary Rusk emphasized that they make absolutely sure the Filipinos fully understood that the American financial concessions, if accepted, did not constitute "an open-ended commitment" of American aid to the Philippines. . . .

All the State Department really accomplished with all the negotiations conducted up through mid-March 1965, was essentially nothing more than an agreement with the Macapagal Administration. The PHILCAG [Philippine Civic Action Group] deployment to Vietnam still could not take place without a Philippine Congress authorization, and getting this authorization in 1965, a Philippine presidential and legislative election year, remained problematic at best. State Department officials, in their desire to get the Macapagal-negotiated agreements implemented, viewed it as America's best interest to support Macapagal in his 1965 presidential campaign against a forceful challenge by Ferdinand Marcos, the Majority Leader of the Philippine Senate. To this end, the Johnson Administration implemented a number of U.S. actions directly designed to benefit the Philippine national economy which would, in turn, increase Macapagal's popularity with the general Philippine population . . .

The November 1965 Philippine elections did not turn out as either Macapagal or the State Department hoped. Unexpectedly, the Filipino voters elected Ferdinand Marcos, who had a long history of opposition to sending Filipino military aid to South Vietnam, as their new president. Washington officials did not, however, permit this detail to impede their pursuit of the PHILCAG detachment. Filipino officials had hardly completed tallying the November ballots when Washington acted. Between December 1965 and January 1966, in addition to almost constant local pressure applied by Ambassador [William] Blair, Lyndon Johnson sent five diplomatic missions, headed by Vice President Hubert Humphrey, Secretary of State Dean Rusk, Senator Mike Mansfield, Ambassador W. Averell Harriman, and General Ed Lansdale, to the Philippines to pressure Marcos into changing his mind about sending Philippine troops to South Vietnam. These American pressure tactics were successful only to a degree. They did manage to persuade Marcos to reverse his position on sending a detachment of Philippine troops to South Vietnam, but Marcos' acquiescence was not total. Marcos felt that, because PHILCAG was only an engineering and civic action detachment, and not a combat unit, he could agree to their deployment without compromising his beliefs and promises made to the Philippine people. Much to Washington's dismay, however, Marcos remained adamant about not sending a Philippine combat unit to Vietnam.

Once Marcos made the decision that sending PHILCAG to South Vietnam would be in the best interests of the Philippines, it became necessary to explain his decision to the Filipinos who had elected him, many of whom had voted against Macapagal because of their objections to any such action. Marcos justified the deployment of PHILCAG by employing essentially the same arguments used by the Macapagal administration, but with one major omission. One of the primary reasons behind his decision, the economic incentives offered by the United States, was not made public. Fearing that he would be accused of being bought by the United States, Marcos deemed it an absolute necessity that the economic benefits the Philippines would derive from sending PHILCAG to South Vietnam be hidden from the Philippine citizenry. Further, he did not want the Filipino general population to know that the

U.S. concessions would also be used to strengthen and extend his power base in the Philippines:

> From the first he had worked on a plan that would modernize the military and extend its influence in the countryside, thus giving the administration a greater capability for governance. There was no way of raising the funds required for this plan internally. Support had to come from the United States...and no such support could possibly be forthcoming to the Philippines unless she helped the United States by a show of support in Viet-Nam. . . .

Despite the large amount of financial aid the United States sent to the Philippines as payment for the PHILCAG deployment, the official record still shows the Philippine government as paying almost all of PHILCAG's expenses in Vietnam. This state of affairs did not, however, occur by happenstance. Because of the Johnson Administration's need to maintain the public image of PHILCAG's being solely a Philippine financed contribution to the More Flags program, the State Department worked diligently to hide almost all American aid arrangements with the Philippines. Washington made sure that the American people would not find out that U.S. funds were being funneled into the Philippine budget to cover PHILCAG's expenses. As a result of these covert arrangements, the public record only shows the U.S. providing a very small amount of the expenses PHILCAG incurred while serving in South Vietnam other than these supplies furnished to all allied troops while they were actually in South Vietnam (such things as transportation, building supplies, arms and ammunition, medical supplies, etc.). . . .

In early 1967, with opposition to PHILCAG growing even from within his own party, Marcos realized that he had no guarantees on getting a 1967–1968 funding authorization through Congress. Consequently, as the original 1966 funding began to run out in July 1967, Marcos elected not to even approach the Philippine legislature for additional monies to keep PHILCAG deployed for another year. Marcos instead chose to utilize the fungible power granted him by Philippine law to continue funding the PHILCAG unit's continued service in Vietnam. An immediate problem developed, however, with this more personal method of financing—the monies Marcos so generated were not sufficient to fund the entire 2,000-man PHILCAG contingent. Marcos was forced, if the funds were to fit the manpower, to reduce PHILCAG personnel in Vietnam. As a direct result of Marcos' new funding methods, then, PHILCAG personnel numbers in Vietnam began falling, from a high of 2,050 in 1966 and 1967 to approximately 1,500 in 1968.

At about the same moment that Marcos undertook his personal financing of PHILCAG, in July 1967, the United States and the Philippines began discussions over a somewhat related issue. By this time, the United States had accepted the fact, however reluctantly, that the Philippines would send no combat units to Vietnam. It appeared, on the surface at least, that PHILCAG, or a unit similar to it, amounted to the maximum aid the United States could expect from the Philippines. However, there remained yet one other slight possibility for the United States to obtain a further Philippine military commitment for Vietnam. Since prior to World War II, it had been possible for Filipino civilians to enlist in the various military branches. Harking back to this long standing military tradition, Marcos Administration officials advanced the idea for a plan that would have 2,000 or more Filipino citizens enlist in the U.S. Army. Then, after training, these enlistees would serve as an all-Filipino combat unit in Vietnam. By the use of such a stratagem, the Marcos government felt that both Philippine and U.S. goals could be achieved: The United States would get another combat unit sent to South Vietnam and the Philippines would receive the substantial economic benefits accruing from their citizens' military service. Nevertheless, despite the idea's advantages to both countries' governments, the suggestion never got past the discussion stage. Policy makers in the United States simply felt the American press and public would not stand for the United States supporting a so patently obvious mercenary unit. . . .

When viewed in retrospect, several contributing factors appear to have played a role in Marcos' first deciding to limit the size of PHILCAG in Vietnam, then to withdraw it completely. As one scholar suggests, Marcos could have simply come to the conclusion that Vietnam was no longer the "key to peace or security in Southeast Asia," and acted to extricate the Philippines from a now questionable situation. Or, as yet another scholar notes, since the U.S. aid already sent to the Philippines constituted a "pay off" for Marcos' support of the American position in South Vietnam, and feeling he had fulfilled his end of the bargain, Marcos felt free to withdraw PHILCAG when and if he saw fit. The most likely reason for Marcos' decision to withdraw PHILCAG from Vietnam, however, was that PHILCAG became an "embarrassment" to him. Support for this contention is found when one examines the evidence brought to light by a series of U.S. Senate subcommittee hearings conducted between 30 September and 3 October 1969. It was these hearings, called to investigate the financial dealings underlying the Philippines More Flags contribution, that most probably served to push Marcos into withdrawing PHILCAG from Vietnam:

> When the Symington hearings . . . made public the extent of American financing, a tremendous crisis of confidence, and a self-perceived loss of face . . . developed in the Philippines. Consequently, President Marcos withdrew the rest of PHILCAG more suddenly than had been anticipated.

It was not, however, the general Filipino population that experienced a "loss of face," it was Ferdinand Marcos himself. In his desire not to be considered a lackey of the United States, Marcos, from the moment he became president, had insisted that all details of the Filipino-American funding negotiations for PHILCAG be hidden from the Philippine public. . . . Because of the Senate hearings, most of the PHILCAG negotiations Marcos wanted kept secret became public knowledge, and he now had to move quickly to minimize their damage. On 14 November 1969, just days after the Senate published the hearing results, Marcos notified the U.S. Embassy in Manila that PHILCAG would soon be withdrawn, and, by 15 December, PHILCAG was gone from Vietnam.

President Marcos was not alone, however, in wanting a shroud of secrecy draped over the details of the Philippines' More Flags contribution. The Johnson Administration also wanted very much to hide their actions in the matter from the American people. In fact, the Americans began hiding their involvement in the funding of a Philippine military commitment to South Vietnam in 1965, even before Marcos was elected president:

> It is highly desirable that the U.S. financial support not be apparent, to avoid lending credence to possible accusations that IMAF personnel are U.S. 'mercenaries.' This will not be a problem with the MAP [Mutual Assistance Program] input, which will come largely as additions to regular programs, but to effectively conceal the U.S. payment of other items of cost the use of unvouchered funds is considered necessary. It is, therefore, proposed that funds be provided as a cash grant to be used in two ways—to pay special overseas allowances and support costs of the contingents in Vietnam and to provide budget support to the Government of the Philippines to enable it to assume the pay and allowances of the replacement troops. . . .

Whatever may or may not have been his reasons for doing so, the fact remains that Ferdinand Marcos did withdraw the PHILCAG detachment from South Vietnam in December 1969. And in so doing, he ended the Philippines' contribution of mercenary troops to the United States' war effort.

The Thai Troop Commitment

Of the five free world nations that sent combat troops to South Vietnam under the auspices of L.B.J.'s More Flags program, only the Kingdom of Thailand physically occupies the Southeast Asian land mass with the countries of the former French Indochina. It can thus be argued that Thailand, of all the free world troop contributing nations, had sound political reasons for becoming militarily involved in the Vietnamese conflict. The validity of this argument, however, rests on a disputed cold war maxim. It can be supported only if one accepts the domino theory and its basic tenet that all of Southeast Asia would likely fall to the communists if South Vietnam fell. For those holding such beliefs then, because of Thailand's singular geographic circumstances, its commitment of combat troops to assist the South Vietnamese was regarded as a justified response to legitimate Thai national interests. An investigation of the documentary record of the motives behind Thailand's sending combat units to Vietnam does not, however, support such an explanation. The Thai military contingent deployed to South Vietnam, as were the Korean and Filipino commitments that preceded it, was a mercenary force bought and paid for by the United States.

. . . the Kennedy Administration was delighted to accede to Bangkok's desires for closer military and political alliances with Washington. Viewing Thailand's national security needs at the time as being coincident with American foreign policy needs for Southeast Asia, the United States began the process of irrevocably linking the Thai government to the American foreign policy positions for the region. In the Rusk-Thanat Treaty of 1962, the first Kennedy Administration move to achieve this end, the United States furnished the Thai government with a guarantee afforded few other American allies, a *unilateral* assurance that America would come to Thailand's defense in case of invasion. Then, following almost immediately its negotiations for the Rusk-Thanat Treaty, the United States demonstrated its support of the Thai government in a more tangible way by sending a battalion of United

States Marines to assist the Thais in patrolling their northern borders. In one final move to tie Thailand to American interests in the region, the Kennedy Administration increased by $50 million the amount of military aid sent to Thailand. . . .

The $50 million increase in American financial aid sent to Thailand in 1963 succeeded in achieving the most immediate U.S. objective Washington sought from its increased diplomatic ties with Thailand. American military experts knew the Thais wanted this aid to finance a strengthening of their internal military defense capabilities. In giving the Thais this money, the United States not only ingratiated itself with the Thai military since this would increase Thailand's own national security posture, but the aid's use in this manner would also succeed in the "creation of a 'war infrastructure' in Thailand." Such developments inside Thailand were felt necessary because, even in the Kennedy Administration, the feeling in Washington was that the conflict then being waged in South Vietnam could easily spill over into Thailand. American military planners thus felt, if such an event transpired, that Thailand's basic military infrastructure needed expanding and modernizing so it would be capable of accepting possible future American military missions. . . .

When an in-depth examination is made into every aspect of the record, a determination of who was manipulating whom becomes difficult to assert. While Thailand may well have been manipulating the United States in 1962 and 1963, after that date, the roles were reversed. Through the high level of American economic assistance over the succeeding years, Washington assured itself that, after 1964, it would do the manipulating. . . .

Even during the early talks between Kennedy Administration officials and the Thais, the relative order of importance Thai officials attached to the items on their agenda perplexed the American diplomats. To the Americans, it only made sense that the escalating war in Vietnam and Laos should be the source of most concern to the Thai government. The Thai government's position was, however, that while they did consider the events occurring along their borders a problem, these events did not top the list. To the Thais, even though communist-led guerrilla raids on Thailand's northeastern provinces were a constant occurrence, they did not look on these activities as presenting a "major internal threat" to Thailand's national security. To the Thai government officials the major threat to their sovereignty came from another source. Feeling "confident that they [could] contain any threats from Indochina alone," the Thai government felt that a direct confrontation with Communist China presented the only real danger. Thai national security concerns then, as reflected in their negotiations with the United States throughout the 1960s, focused on questions of how Thailand could best defend itself against Red China. To these Thai government officials, because of their abiding fear of a direct confrontation with the Communist Chinese, it became absolutely mandatory for Thailand to maintain a close military and political alliance with the United States, no matter the cost. . . .

As much as they could, then, American diplomats in Bangkok used the uneasy stability of the Thai government to further U.S. interests in the country and the region. The base fact that the Thai government was not democratic, however, never prejudiced the State Department's dealings with the Thai leadership. American officials would not allow the knowledge that U.S. economic and military aid was being used by the Thai government leaders "to maintain and consolidate their military control of Thailand" to interfere with American designs for the region. Still, even though this use of American aid was perfectly acceptable to both Kennedy and Johnson administration policymakers, Thai government exigencies necessitated a very careful crafting of the physical contents of any U.S. aid to Thailand. Such aid had to serve, in effect, two sometimes dichotomous purposes: it first and foremost had to furnish tangible American support for the upper-echelon military leaders who controlled the government, while at the same time furnishing support for the second-echelon of military officers, the traditional breeding ground for Thai governmental coups. This second requirement for American aid was deemed an absolute necessity for, as American diplomats feared, if U.S. aid did not adequately placate this lower level of the Thai military, these officers might "very well resume their normal concentration on how to overthrow the present regime." It is thus understandable that, with almost all Thai-American relations being focused on bolstering the various levels of Thailand's military establishment, it was military aid, not domestic aid, which became the dominant type of American aid sent to Thailand during this period. . . .

In addition to the possible effects a U.S. request for Thai [combat] troops might have on the stability of the Thai government, [U.S. Ambassador to Thailand Graham] Martin also perceived another very valid reason for Secretary Rusk not to pursue the matter further [in 1965]. Such an American troop request at this time would potentially endanger other, even more militarily critical, Thai-U.S. negotiations then in their earliest stages. These arguments proved convincing, as

Secretary Rusk ultimately chose not to take this opportunity to submit a request for a Thai commitment of combat troops. To Rusk, and Secretary of Defense McNamara, the American-Thai negotiations mentioned by Ambassador Martin, involving receiving permission to base American B-52s in Thailand, constituted a more important issue at that particular moment: "The push for a great increase in the Thai troop commitment…[had to wait] until after the Americans had gained the right to base B-52s in Thailand."…

Until 1966, geographical considerations alone served as the rationale for the Thai government's becoming militarily involved in America's war in Indochina. Throughout this early period, both the United States and Thai governments felt that any direct Thai involvement in the conflict should be limited to actions inside the territories of countries contiguous to Thailand, in Cambodia and Laos. Neither the U.S. nor Thai government thought that a Thai military role in South Vietnam was either necessary or even particularly desirable. Thai government officials had, in fact, made it clear to the United States as early as August 1964, that while they were willing to send their soldiers into Laos, they would not even consider sending troops to Vietnam. It would appear then, if the official Thai government position on not sending troops to Vietnam is coupled with the known antipathy of the Thai junior officer corps to such a move, that there existed little possibility of the United States' obtaining a More Flags troop commitment from Thailand. Yet, such was not the case. In late 1966, United States and Thai negotiators began discussions on what it would take for the Johnson Administration to convince the Thai government to send a Thai combat unit to Vietnam.

There is no currently available documentation that offers an explanation of why the Thai government chose to abandon its long-standing position on sending combat troops to Vietnam. The record simply states that, despite his "not really wish [ing] to send troops to Vietnam," Thai Prime Minister Thanom [Kittikachorn] announced to the world through a press conference held on 6 January 1967, that Thailand would dispatch a "ground force to take an active part in the fighting in South Vietnam." Washington had received its first notification that Thailand had agreed to send "a reinforced Thai Battalion to fight in Viet-Nam" three days earlier, on 3 January 1967.

Since U.S. and Thai negotiators had already begun formal discussions on deploying a Thai combat force to Vietnam in 1966, Thanom's January 1967 announcement did not come as a surprise to U.S. government insiders. Still, even while some U.S. officials knew ahead of time that

Thanom was leaning toward a deployment of Thai troops, they also knew that Thanom had one major problem to overcome before he could publicly announce any troop deployment to South Vietnam. Thanom may have agreed to deploy these troops, but this did not by itself solve the problem of Thai junior officer corps opposition. Events of 30 December 1966, however, succeeded in significantly reducing Thanom's worries that this opposition would occur, or at least led him to believe that if opposition did arise, it would be minimal. On this date, four Bangkok newspapers simultaneously published stories on the possibility of Thailand's deploying an all-volunteer combat force to South Vietnam. The immediate public response to these articles was almost universal support for the idea, and Prime Minister Thanom had the support he needed to overcome any junior officer objections. If there were any grumblings in the ranks after Thanom's 6 January commitment of Thai troops, they quickly dissipated in the flood of public support that followed Thanom's announcement. The idea of sending Thai soldiers to Vietnam became so popular that, by the end of January 1967, more than 5,000 men in Bangkok alone volunteered to serve in any unit deployed there. . . .

Supposedly, because of its all-volunteer composition, the deployment of this first Thai combat detachment to Vietnam (which became known as the Queen's Cobras) had to be delayed until the regiment completed an extensive training period. At least this provided the official excuse for why the unit did not begin arriving in Vietnam until late September 1967, almost eight months after its being formally organized as the Royal Thai Army Volunteer Regiment (RTAVR). This explanation for the deployment delay is not supported by the evidence, however, since 97 percent of the Queen's Cobras personnel were not untrained volunteers but regular Thai Army soldiers. While the regiment did require some specialized training, organizational, logistical, and supply problems were the main reasons for the unit's delay in arriving in Vietnam.

With the Thai government finally agreeing to a commitment of combat troops to South Vietnam, the floodgates for further U.S. troop requests were opened. Johnson Administration officials now felt that no obstacle remained to hamper their pursuit of even more Thai troops for Vietnam, and they moved quickly to take advantage of their freedom of action. The first contingents of the Queen's Cobras had not even begun arriving in South Vietnam when the United States, in the form of a special presidential mission headed by Clark Clifford and Maxwell Taylor, began pressing the Thais for an even larger military commitment.

Officially, the purpose of the Clifford-Taylor 22 July to 5 August 1967 mission was to apprise the leaders of the allied troop-contributing nations of current and future U.S. actions in South Vietnam. The two presidential envoys had other, furtive, presidential instructions, however. President Johnson also charged Clifford and Taylor with the responsibility of soliciting each allied leader to increase the numbers of their combat troops committed to Vietnam.

Despite the Thai agreement to commit the Queen's Cobras to Vietnam, Ambassador Martin still felt that their actions were fraught with danger, both for Thailand and for the United States. Thus, when Clifford and Taylor arrived in Thailand, Ambassador Martin hoped to convince them of the inadvisability of making a further military request of the Thais. In an embassy briefing arranged to prepare Clifford and Taylor for their discussions with Prime Minister Thanom, Ambassador Martin reiterated his earlier advice to Secretary of State Rusk—that Thailand's major contribution to the Vietnamese War effort lay in continuing its covert activities in Laos, not by sending more troops to South Vietnam. Ambassador Martin's advice was not, however, what Clark Clifford wanted to hear:

> Clifford made it briefly and pithily clear that he wanted to hear no more such talk. What the President wanted was more troops in South Vietnam. Because the President had done everything to support Thailand, the President now expected Thailand to support him. The need was in South Vietnam and that was where the President wanted Thai forces.

President Johnson wanted more troops from Thailand, and more troops from Thailand were what he was going to get.

Official negotiations for the deployment of a much larger Thai troop contribution to South Vietnam began soon after the Clifford-Taylor mission left Bangkok, with "the Thai digging in their heels in order to get everything possible." The forceful demands made by the Thai negotiators did not, however, come as a surprise to the Americans. American diplomats knew that the Thai government recognized the base realities behind the U.S. requests for more troops: that the United States needed additional Thai troops for political reasons, and not to meet any perceived needs of the Vietnamese government. Nevertheless, even though the American negotiators knew the Thais recognized the real reasons for the U.S. requests, they also knew that Thailand had been made so obligated to U.S. interests by 1967—militarily, economically, and politically—that it was no longer possible for them to refuse outright the U.S. demand for more Thai troops.

Thai diplomats, then, entered the 1967 negotiations holding few illusions that Saigon really needed their troops. Although Thailand had already committed more than 2,000 men to fight in South Vietnam, Thai diplomats knew full well that these young men had been sent to fight and die in an American war for American needs. Still, by 1967, these Thai officials also knew that they had few options available but to comply with American demands. While Thai Foreign Minister Thanat Khoman would later lament his country's acquiescence, he still recognized there was not much more he or his country could do at the time:

> The situation worsened when the United States, feeling lonely in Viet-Nam, began to induce other countries . . . to get into the quagmire that she was, to a certain extent, responsible for creating. . . . Thailand, *at the U.S. insistence* [emphasis added], had to send a full division of 12,000 men to join the American GI's.

Although State Department officials considered it an all but foregone conclusion in 1967 that Thailand would send more troops to Vietnam, questions on how much the United States would have to pay for these troops still remained undecided. And if Thai government officials felt that the Americans were forcing them into backing a U.S. policy position that might not be in Thailand's own best interests, at least these negotiators knew Thailand could reap economic rewards for their troops' services. Knowing of the liberal concessions the State Department had already made to the Koreans and the Filipinos for their troop commitments, Thai officials entered the negotiations with the Americans prepared to insist on as many U.S. concessions as possible. . . .

After an obligatory give-and-take at the negotiating table, Thailand agreed to accept a seven point concession package which obligated the United States to:

1. Pay all training costs for the 10,000 man unit sent to South Vietnam;
2. Supply all equipment for the 10,000 men, equipment that the Thai government would keep when the Thai forces withdrew from South Vietnam;
3. Pay all of the costs of overseas allowances over and above their base pay and allowances;

4. Supply all equipment for the rotational troops during their training period, with Thailand retaining this equipment;
5. Provide a HAWK anti-aircraft battery and the training of Thai personnel to man it, for deployment inside Thailand;
6. Increase the Mutual Assistance Program (MAP) contributions for Fiscal Year (FY) '68 from $60 million to $75 million; and
7. Increase the planned MAP contributions for FY '69 from $60 million to $75 million. . . .

It would appear, when a comparison is made of the list of American concessions obtained by the Thais for their troops with those obtained by the Koreans and the Filipinos, that the Thais received substantially less U.S. aid for their combat forces than did the other two countries. Such was not the case, however. Inherent in the aforementioned list of American concessions, but not readily apparent, were two major and continuing sources of U.S. aid to the Thai military that succeeded in bringing the amount of U.S. aid to Thailand into a rough parity with that going to South Korea and the Philippines.

The first of these additional benefits derived from the aid agreement components that had the United States supplying all the military equipment for both the Thai troops actually serving in Vietnam and for those troops training inside Thailand for future rotation to Vietnam. The significance of these concessions becomes clear when the total size of Thailand's armed forces is added into the equation. At the height of Thailand's military commitment to South Vietnam, approximately 14 percent of the entire Thai armed forces were serving there. Thus, when the United States agreement to furnish all the equipment to this 14 percent is coupled to its agreement to similarly equip the Thai troops in training, it becomes clear that Thailand was receiving a very large amount of U.S. aid. These two concessions alone amount to, in effect, the United States guaranteeing the Thai military a continuing resupply of new military equipment for almost a third of the entire Thai armed forces. A direct result of this situation would have been, if Thailand had kept their troops in South Vietnam for several years, that the United States would eventually have provided a complete reequipment of the entire Thai armed forces.

A second major benefit accruing to the Thai military lay in the financial incentives the United States supplied, the payment "of the costs of overseas allowances" for every Thai soldier serving in Vietnam. These

U.S. funded overseas allowances . . . succeeded in more than doubling each Thai soldier's salary. . . .

In addition to these direct monetary incentives, any Thai soldier who maintained a satisfactory war record while serving in South Vietnam could continue to draw his combat pay for the rest of his military career. Plus, every day a career soldier spent in Vietnam counted double for retirement purposes. Combat duty in Vietnam also proved especially advantageous to the career advancement of Thailand's upper and second echelon leadership corps. It seems that, to the Thai military high command, their 12,000-man division serving in Vietnam required the leadership of ten generals and 11 full colonels. That this constituted a grossly inflated command structure becomes evident when the Thai division is compared with an U.S. division. . . .

. . . In late July 1968, the first elements of the Royal Thai Army Expeditionary Division (RTAED), also known as the Black Panthers, began arriving in South Vietnam as the Queen's Cobras' replacements. Although the two units never served together in Vietnam, because of the Thai government's duplication of the American schedule of only having their troops serve a year's tour of duty in Vietnam, many of the Queen's Cobras eventually returned to Vietnam to serve with the Black Panthers.

The deployment of the Black Panthers to Vietnam represented Thailand's final More Flags troop contribution. By the time the final members of the division arrived in Vietnam on 9 January 1969, Lyndon Johnson had only 11 days left in power and thus could not pressure the Thais further for an even larger troop commitment. Still, even though President Johnson soon left office, Thailand elected not to remove their troops. Thai troops continued to serve in South Vietnam until 1972, leaving only a scant few months before the last American troops departed.

The fact that Thailand kept their troops in Vietnam almost to the very end, when coupled with Thailand's having a closely held interest in the outcome of their neighbor's conflict, would seem to cast doubt on any allegation that the Thai troops in Vietnam served as American mercenaries. After all, Thailand, unlike South Korea and the Philippines, did have its national borders directly threatened by the war then raging in Vietnam. One can argue, then, and Thailand's government did so maintain, that in order to avoid having the conflict spread to its own territory, Thailand had to commit its troops to fight in South Vietnam.

This argument constitutes, however, only a simple after-the-fact justification. Records clearly indicate that the Thai government did not perceive the conflict in South Vietnam as a direct threat to their national sovereignty. To the Thais, only a direct confrontation with Red China could do that. The record also presents ample evidence that Thai government leaders did not want to commit their troops to South Vietnam and, indeed, had a long history of resistance to any such suggestion that they do so. It is thus evident that, until 1967, the Thai government felt that sending their troops to fight in South Vietnam was not in the Thai national interest. However, the fact still remains that they did just that.

When all the evidence is examined, it becomes clear that the Thai troop contingent to Vietnam became an American mercenary operation when the Thai government insisted that the United States make very substantial financial concessions for their deployment.

B. Pakistani Opposition

*Robert McMahon**

Reaping the Whirlwind

. . . As [Pakistani Foreign Secretary Zulfikar Ali] Bhutto so forthrightly acknowledged, Pakistan's overture toward China derived not from any ideological affinity for its communist neighbor. Instead, it represented diplomatic pragmatism of the highest order. Obsessed with the potential danger posed to their nation's security by a larger and more powerful India, Pakistani policymakers believed that an entente with China provided a greater degree of protection than their Western alliances alone could offer. Born of small-power insecurity conjoined with a deepening skepticism about the reliability of its principal ally, Pakistan's opening toward China serves as a classic case of geopolitical expediency overcoming ideological dissonance.

From Washington's perspective, however, the opening stood as an egregious provocation. It violated the bedrock assumptions undergirding all of America's Cold War alliances. Further, it conferred a degree of respectability on what American policymakers contemptuously regarded as an outlaw state. The Kennedy administration's military commitment to India, after all, was driven primarily by American concern about the threat China posed to the noncommunist nations of South and Southeast Asia. In the view of American national security planners, China had become a near-demonic force in world affairs; the Sino-Soviet split, they were convinced, had just emboldened Beijing's leaders, making them more, rather than less, aggressive, adventuristic, and unpredictable. . . .

. . . Kennedy, Johnson, and their senior aides ranked the containment of China as one of the overriding objectives of U.S. foreign policy. Kennedy's fixation with India's importance to the United States flowed largely from his belief in the salience of India to that crucial goal. Pakistan's China gambit infuriated Johnson, as it had Kennedy, because it threatened to undermine that goal. . . .

. . . News of the Indo-American military assistance pact [in June 1964] unleashed a floodtide of anti-American demonstrations throughout the country [of Pakistan]. The knowledge that the United States was deliberately delaying future military aid commitments to Pakistan as a crude form of punishment for its China policy fueled the intensity of those protests. Pakistan's leaders found the differential treatment meted out by its erstwhile ally in Washington to a formally nonaligned state especially galling. U.S. policy is "based on opportunism and is devoid of moral quality," [Pakistani President] Ayub [Khan] snapped during a press interview; "now Americans do not hesitate to let down their friends." The Pakistani leader also registered a vigorous, formal protest, notifying Johnson in a letter of July 7 that Pakistan might now have to reappraise its commitments to SEATO and CENTO.

The quick-tempered Johnson was infuriated by the curt tone of Ayub's message and by the veiled threat that it contained. In a meeting with Ambassador Ghulam Ahmed, who personally delivered the letter to him, Johnson made no effort to hide his "considerable distress" with Ayub's unjustified complaints. Offering the standard defense of U.S. policy, he insisted that military aid to India served American—and Pakistani—interests by contributing to the containment of the communist threat to the subcontinent. It hardly offered proof that Washington was being "disloyal" to its Pakistani ally, as Ayub charged. The president turned the charge around. He implied that Pakistan, by dint of its relationship with China, was the real disloyal partner, especially in view of the grave threat that China currently posed to the noncommunist states of Southeast Asia. LBJ told the ambassador flatly that if Pakistan chose to reexamine its relationship with the United States, regrettable as it might be, the United States would have no choice but to reexamine its relationship with Pakistan. . . .

. . . The United States should take no action to placate the Pakistanis at this juncture, Johnson directed; he wanted a cooling-off period instead, during which U.S.-Pakistani relations would remain correct but aloof. LBJ instructed [U.S. Ambassador to Pakistan Walter] McConaughy, upon the latter's return to Karachi, to inform Ayub personally of his candid remarks to Ahmed, stress the "worrisome implications for the future" of the Pakistani-Chinese relationship, emphasize American concern with the threat of Chinese subversion and aggression in Southeast Asia, and impress upon Ayub the importance Washington attached to Pakistan joining the "free world effort in Viet Nam and at least show[ing the] flag there. . . .

Born of frustration and anger, Johnson's confrontation with Ahmed and his blunt follow-up message to Ayub set the tone for U.S.-Pakistani relations over the next six months. It was a troubled and stormy period that witnessed a further acceleration of the trends first set in motion by the Chinese invasion of India in October 1962. Pakistan expanded its ties with many of the nonaligned states of Asia and Africa, making a special effort to warm up to Sukarno's Indonesia, continued to pursue actively a closer connection with China, and steadily deemphasized its commitments to SEATO and CENTO. For its part, the United States maintained a cordial but distant relationship with its recalcitrant ally. When the pro-American Finance Minister Mohammed Shoaib visited Washington in September 1964, [National Security Advisor McGeorge] Bundy reminded him that fundamental differences over China posed the greatest obstacle to a constructive dialogue between Washington and Karachi. The deepening crisis in South Vietnam during this same period, which preoccupied Johnson and his senior aides, just exacerbated U.S.-Pakistani tensions. As the Johnson administration moved to shore up the embattled Saigon regime, many of its leading analysts saw Beijing, more than either Hanoi or the Viet Cong guerrillas, as America's real foe in Southeast Asia. . . .

In order to reopen the stalled dialogue with Pakistan, in January 1965 Johnson approved a State Department recommendation that he invite Ayub to visit Washington that April. Johnson envisioned the meeting as an opportunity to persuade the Pakistani leader that, despite the chill that had beset Pakistani-American relations since July, a "basis for close and mutually beneficial ties" between the two countries continued to exist. He also intended to discuss frankly with Ayub the alarming gap that separated U.S. and Pakistani assessments of Chinese actions and intentions. The State Department held relatively modest hopes for the visit. . . .

Just nine days before the Pakistani leader's arrival in Washington, to the shock and dismay and some of his own advisers, Johnson abruptly withdrew his invitation. The recent state visits by Ayub to Moscow and Beijing, especially the latter trip, lay behind the president's precipitous action. Much to Johnson's discomfiture, Ayub had greeted [Chinese leaders] Mao [Zedong], Zhou [Enlai], and their compatriots with open arms. He had pledged "lasting friendship and fruitful cooperation" between Pakistan and China, openly criticized the escalation of the American commitment in Vietnam, and, according to a State Department intelligence assessment, even adopted "Afro-Asian jargon" in his speeches. That "disturbing" behavior irritated and angered the thin-skinned Johnson. On April 6 he told his senior aides that Ayub's arrival in Washington would just focus attention on the Pakistani's unfortunate behavior and unfriendly statements in the two communist capitals, thus jeopardizing congressional action on the administration's foreign aid bill. In addition, Ayub would almost certainly feel compelled to make statements regarding Vietnam that would spark additional controversy with Congress and with the media.

In an explanatory letter to the surprised Ayub, Johnson pulled few punches. After the obligatory professions of goodwill, the president came right to the point. He said that his long years of experience with Congress led him "to the conclusion that your visit at this time would focus public attention on the differences between Pakistani and United States policy toward Communist China." Such an airing of differences, at the very moment that Congress was deliberating about the administration's foreign aid budget proposals, might "gravely affect" continued legislative support for Pakistan's development and defense efforts. "I cannot overstate the full depth of American feeling about Communist China," Johnson wrote. "The mounting number of American casualties in South Vietnam is having a profound effect upon American opinion. This is being felt in Congress just at the time when our foreign aid legislation is at the most sensitive point in the legislative cycle." Under the circumstances, Johnson concluded, a postponement of the visit until the fall, when it would likely generate less heat, appeared the wisest course of action.

In order to maintain a rough parallelism in U.S. treatment of India and Pakistan, Johnson at the very same time postponed the first scheduled visit to the United States of the new Indian prime minister, Lal Bahadur Shastri. . . .

Both Ayub and Shastri expressed indignation at the abrupt cancellation of their invitations. . . .

Once again, however, [National Security Council aide Robert] Komer seriously underestimated the impact of American heavy-handedness on the two countries—and on Indo-Pakistani relations. Johnson's announcement proved especially ill-timed in the latter regard since at the very moment of his notification to Ayub and Shastri large-scale clashes between Indian and Pakistani troops were taking place. The clashes occurred in a desolate area abutting the Arabian Sea called the Rann of Kutch. India and Pakistan maintained overlapping border claims there, the symbolic significance of which far outweighed any material or strategic value either side attached to the land in question. The use by Pakistani troops of U.S.-supplied weapons raised awkward political questions for the United States. The fighting "has propelled us once more into the center of a subcontinental dispute," a State Department analysis noted, "at a moment when our leverage in both countries is at a low point." Pakistan, it speculated, may have precipitated the conflict in the hope that its use of U.S. military equipment would drive a wedge between India and the United States. If that was the Pakistani intention, the ploy proved quite effective. Almost immediately, India lodged a vehement protest with the United States, reminding Washington of its repeated assurances that it would not allow Pakistan to use U.S. military equipment against India. [Chester] Bowles urgently cabled the State Department that its response to this troubling affair would have a far-reaching effect on U.S.-Indian relations.

Under the circumstances, the Johnson administration believed it had no choice but to inform Pakistan and India that it was prohibiting the use of any U.S. military materiel in the Rann. Pakistanis deeply resented this edict, castigating it as yet another American capitulation to India. They considered the U.S. decision to prohibit the use by either side of its military equipment to be grossly unfair since virtually all of Pakistan's equipment came from the United States whereas India acquired military hardware from a variety of sources. Foreign Minister Bhutto warned that the U.S. decision would have profoundly negative repercussions on Pakistani-American relations.

The Rann of Kutch incident, although militarily insignificant, did have important diplomatic consequences. In its aftermath, confidence in the United States plummeted in both Rawalpindi and New Delhi—simultaneously. Shastri and his chief advisers, already stung by Johnson's disinvitation, felt betrayed by Pakistan's use of American equipment. America's repeated promises to them that it would deter Pakistani aggression now appeared empty. For their part, Pakistani leaders had their gravest suspicions confirmed by the U.S. response to the

Rann of Kutch fighting; they were now convinced that previous U.S. pledges about restraining Indian aggression were meaningless. Its standing with the two parties was now so low that the United States lacked sufficient leverage to play even a minor mediatory role. Accordingly, it deferred to Great Britain, which managed to negotiate a cease-fire agreement that Ayub and Shastri signed in London on June 30. The Johnson administration could do little but applaud the British effort from the sidelines.

Another leader might have sought to rebuild bridges at such an incendiary juncture. Not Lyndon Johnson. Convinced that any conciliatory moves could be read as a sign of weakness, Johnson opted instead to intensify American pressure on both Pakistan and India. Late in April, while the skirmishes in the Rann were still raging, he directed that all pending aid decisions regarding the two countries first be cleared with the White House. "The President's reluctance to move forward on India and Pakistan matters," Komer explained, "stems from his own deep instinct that we are not getting enough for our massive investment in either." . . .

. . . Additionally, he requested State and AID [Agency for International Development] to conduct a full-scale review of all U.S. economic aid programs to India and Pakistan in order to determine "(a) whether the US should be spending such large sums in either country; and (b) how to achieve more leverage for our money, in terms both of more effective self-help and of our political purposes." . . .

According to an understated assessment by the State Department's intelligence bureau: "Pakistan apparently considers the postponement of the Consortium pledging session [for economic aid to Pakistan] as a major crisis in U.S.-Pakistani relations, and Ayub has probably come to believe that the U.S. intends to use economic aid as a lever to force modifications of Pakistan foreign policy." In fact, Pakistani disillusionment with the United States went far deeper than American analysts recognized. LBJ had deliberately driven Ayub into a corner in the vain hope that increased pressure would bring him around to the American point of view. But Johnson's heavy-handed tactics failed to produce the desired effect. Tensions between the two nations just continued to escalate throughout the summer of 1965, making it difficult for the United States even to keep open its channels of communication with Pakistan.

Crisis Over Kashmir, 1965

At this dangerous juncture, with U.S.-Pakistani misunderstanding at an all-time high, American policymakers were suddenly faced with the most serious threat to the peace of the subcontinent since 1948. The crisis built slowly throughout August 1965, following Ayub's decision early that month to infiltrate Pakistani irregular forces into Indian-occupied Kashmir. Most likely, Ayub sought to undermine the efforts of the Shastri government to integrate the portions of Kashmir that it occupied more fully into the Indian state. He probably calculated that by bringing the Kashmir problem to a head once more Pakistan could at least force India back to the bargaining table. Whatever Ayub's precise motivations, his high-stakes game soon backfired. India moved quickly to block Pakistani infiltration routes, leaving Ayub little choice but to up the ante by sending in regular army forces. On September 1 Pakistani armed forces invaded the extreme southern portion of Kashmir in the Chhamb sector. The drive, which featured the use of U.S.-supplied Patton tanks, aimed at severing the thin communications links between Indian-held Kashmir and India proper. UN Secretary-General U Thant that same day issued an urgent appeal for a cease-fire and for the withdrawal of all armed personnel behind the previous cease-fire line established by the UN. At Johnson's directive, Arthur Goldberg, the U.S. ambassador to the United Nations, immediately endorsed the secretary-general's appeal. . . .

On September 6 the conflict entered a new and more dangerous phase as four Indian divisions thrust across the international boundary in the Punjab, driving toward Lahore. Ayub immediately called in McConaughy to inform him of the Indian violation of Pakistan's territorial integrity. He presented the American ambassador with an aide-memoire that called upon Washington to uphold the 1959 agreement between the United States and Pakistan and act immediately to "suppress and vacate" the Indian aggression.

With the conflict rapidly escalating, Johnson and his top advisers realized that they could not long postpone a decision on U.S. arms shipments to the two warring countries. Former Vice-President [Richard] Nixon, Republican Congressman Gerald R. Ford of Michigan, and Democratic Senator Frank Church of Idaho were among the most prominent politicians who called upon Johnson to terminate immediately all U.S. assistance to both India and Pakistan. . . . "It will certainly be highly resented in both India and Pakistan," Komer acknowledged, "and risks pushing both even further off the deep end. On the other hand, it may well help bring home to both the consequences of their folly.". . .

. . . The Johnson Administration, already seeking to contain the communist threat to Asia with a rapidly expanding contingent of American ground forces in Vietnam, viewed the possibility of a Chinese military thrust into South Asia with extreme wariness. Chinese intervention in the Indo-Pakistani war could pose a challenge of global dimensions to American interests and to American credibility.

Johnson, in response to this frightening new twist, directed American policy along several parallel tracks. First, he ordered the Defense and State Departments to prepare military contingency plans for his review. Those plans presumably were to focus on U.S. military options in the event that a Chinese attack occurred and Indian security became endangered. Second, he pledged continued diplomatic support for U Thant's efforts to bring about a cease-fire. Those efforts culminated on September 20 with a Security Council resolution that called upon the two parties to halt all military operations by September 22 and to begin withdrawing their forces to the positions occupied before the current fighting began. Third, LBJ sought to use whatever influence the United States still retained with New Delhi and Rawalpindi to gain their compliance with the UN resolution. Prompt Indian and Pakistani acceptance of the Security Council directive would, in the view of American experts, serve U.S. interests by obviating the rationale for Chinese involvement.

Firm Pakistani resistance frustrated the American strategy. Although India, flushed with success on the battlefield, readily agreed to accept a cease-fire, Pakistan initially rebuffed the UN resolution. A Chinese decision to postpone the deadline they had arbitrarily imposed on India until midnight, September 22, only partially eased the sense of impending crisis. The Johnson administration feared that Pakistan's defiance of the UN order might yet encourage Chinese intervention. Consequently, upon urgent instructions from Washington, McConaughy forcefully lectured Ayub about the risks he was running. The American ambassador warned Ayub that Pakistan now faced a critical choice: if it should directly or indirectly encourage Chinese entry into the conflict, Pakistan would alienate itself from the West, perhaps permanently. This was not a threat, McConaughy stressed, but a reality.

After an awkward period of wavering, punctuated by additional U.S. pressure, Ayub on September 22 reluctantly acceded to the UN's cease-fire proposal. Given the difficult military prospects that Pakistani forces faced, Ayub almost certainly reasoned that the cease-fire represented the best Pakistan could expect under the circumstances. At least it avoided a complete break with the West which would have only served to heighten Pakistan's isolation and its dependence on an external patron—in that case, ironically, China. Nonetheless, that calculation of realpolitik did not diminish Pakistani fury with the United States. Indeed, Pakistan's leaders and its masses were swept by an unprecedented tide of anti-Americanism. During a "stiff" meeting with the American ambassador on September 29, Ayub sharply upbraided the United States for its revocation of solemn pledges regarding defense support; decried the lack of cooperation by the United States and the lack of appreciation for Pakistani efforts to moderate Chinese policy toward Vietnam; and accused the United States of "bullying" a friendly nation. A series of widespread anti-American demonstrations in Pakistan, including the stoning of the U.S. embassy, the burning of an USIS library, and mob attacks on the U.S. consulate in Lahore, provided stark testimony to the depth of anti-American sentiment in Pakistan. . . .

Johnson, infuriated with the image of self-defeating fratricidal strife presented by the 1965 war, was certain that a different approach to South Asia was long overdue. The conflict embarrassed LBJ politically at the very time that he was seeking public and congressional backing for the expanded U.S. military effort in Vietnam. The unwillingness of either India or Pakistan to stand by the United States in Vietnam or to offer more than the most tepid support for what Johnson invariably portrayed as a defensive response to communist aggression further soured him on the South Asian powers. . . .

Johnson soon conveyed to the Indians and the Pakistanis the fundamental shift that the war had induced in U.S. thinking about South Asia. The president met with Ayub in Washington in December 1965 and made clear to the Pakistani ruler that the alliance between the United States and Pakistan was now over. How soon the United States might resume economic aid and what kind of a relationship could be resurrected out of the ashes of the war with India were questions for the future. Plainly, it would bear little resemblance to the alliance of the past. A blunt Johnson told Ayub that the resolution of those issues would hinge to a great extent on Pakistan's willingness to curtail its ties to China. Much to Johnson's delight, the Pakistani president pursued a statesmanlike approach at the Tashkent negotiations . . . in January 1966 that brought the Indo-Pakistani war to a close. Two months later the president met with newly appointed Indian Prime Minister Indira Gandhi in Washington; Nehru's daughter had just replaced the late Shastri, whose untimely death occurred just one day after he signed the Tashkent agreement. As he had during his earlier sessions with Ayub, Johnson emphasized to the Indian leader that the old relationship between Washington and New Delhi was now over. . . .

The United States now sought a dramatically lowered profile in the subcontinent. Johnson insisted upon more modest and more circumscribed relationships both with India and with Pakistan—relationships consistent with the diminished value of two nations that once again appeared tangential to core American security interests.

Discussion Questions: Asian Allies

1. Was the Johnson Administration justified in using and paying for South Korean, Filipino, and Thai troops in Vietnam?

2. What reasons for using these troops did President Johnson give to the public? Why did he use them?

3. What reasons did the South Korean, Philippine, and Thai governments give for sending troops to Vietnam? Why did each send troops?

4. What events led South Korea to send no further troops? What events led Philippine President Marcos to withdraw troops?

5. Why did Pakistan oppose the Vietnam War?

6. What primary sources might you use to discover more about perspectives of an Asian or Pacific Rim country on the War?

II. European SEATO Allies: British Diplomatic Support, French Opposition

*Caroline Page**

European Perspectives

In general terms European governments were well aware that West European security and the political and military status quo in Europe was underwritten by NATO and the American military presence in Europe. Furthermore, with the exception of France, most European governments considered that Europe was the natural and proper focus for American attention and therefore the increasing U.S. absorption in the Vietnam War was perceived as a threat to Europe, involving as it did a diminution in U.S. interest in the European arena and concentration on Southeast Asia. For though the period of the coldest relations between East and West was over by 1965 and there had been a degree of thawing since the Cuban missile crisis in 1962, nevertheless the relationship between the two "blocs" still involved tensions, and Europe was still the seat of seemingly intractable and continuing political problems with international implications, such as the division of Germany, the post-war borders, and the political position of Berlin; and of course for these reasons and others the world's two opposing major military alliances were focused on Europe.

Thus the attitude of European governments to the U.S. involvement in Vietnam, viewing it as peripheral to the "real" political concerns, is understandable. But by the same token, because the world was still divided into East and West and two opposing ideological blocs it was also possible to perceive, and more importantly to portray, the Vietnam War as an episode in the continuing fight against communist expansionism—an episode that was taking place in a different geographical arena, but that was still a part of the same general problem that faced Europe. There was, therefore, an inherent tension in European government perceptions of the U.S. involvement in South Vietnam, which was only containable so long as the war was perceived (or said to be perceived) as the U.S. portrayed it—in this international framework of Sino-Soviet communist expansion, which, if not halted in Vietnam, would eventually threaten the Western world. This, then, was the link in U.S. propaganda between Southeast Asia and Europe. . . .

The United Kingdom, 1965–1966

Turning first to the more positive aspects of U.K.-U.S. relations, and thus elements that would aid U.S. propagandists, one of the most important factors influencing the British Government during this era was the "special relationship" between Britain and America. Although the warmth of this relationship has varied considerably in different periods, nevertheless in the 1960s British policy-makers acted on the assumption that a "special relationship" did exist, indeed, Prime Minister Harold Wilson [Labour Party] took special pains to nurture the relationship . . . Thus, because of this orientation towards America (and regardless of later attempts to join the Common Market), U.S. propagandists could expect to encounter a more sympathetic climate in British official circles than they might in other countries. In addition, the close economic relationship that Prime Minister Wilson desired certainly did materialize: the British economy was heavily dependent on American support, primarily to avoid any devaluation of sterling. . . .

. . . The fact that Britain's economy was underwritten to such a large extent by America underlined the latter's role of senior partner in the relationship, with America obviously wielding the greater amount of influence and leverage. Wilson, however, had hopes that British support for America in Vietnam would confer the ability to exercise some influence over U.S. policy in Vietnam. Despite being made aware at the earliest stages of escalation of the war that the U.S. had no intention of being swayed by its British ally, Wilson nonetheless persevered for some considerable time on these lines . . .

The accession to power in 1964 of the Labour Party with Harold Wilson as Prime Minister was . . . a particular boon to the Americans, in that the Labour government could support the U.S. without being instantly labelled war-mongering or neo-colonialist. Had the Conservatives been in power it would have been more difficult for them—being identified with the Right—to support the Americans in Vietnam, had they been so inclined. As it was, the Labour government, securely identified with peaceful international traditions, rendered what assistance it wished to the Americans. In addition, Wilson was initially aided in his policy of supporting the U.S. by the fact that the first Labour government had a majority of only five in the House of Commons. This slender majority tended to define the limit of Labour MPs'—even left-wing Labour MPs'—opposition in the House to the government's policies, since rebellion could have led to an unnecessarily early general election. . . .

Concerning U.S. war methods, the British experience of bombing during the Second World War did pose some difficulties for U.S. propagandists. For, according to National Opinion Polls (NOP) in July 1966, although the British public thought the bombing of military targets in North Vietnam was justified, the public emphatically disapproved of any bombing of civilian targets. And this view was expressed when military targets around Hanoi and Haiphong—near the civilian population—had been bombed for the very first time (NOP, July 1966 and Gallup Poll, July 1966). Interestingly, during the early period of the war (1965–66), apart from general questions on support for American policy or "American armed action" in Vietnam, neither of the major polling organizations (NOP and Gallup) in Britain investigated public reaction to U.S. bombing in South Vietnam, where civilian casualties in 1966 were already much higher. . . .

Officially the British Government viewed the U.S. bombing campaign as a legitimate method of fighting the war, and having assured the U.S. Administration of support for the conflict it seemed unlikely that U.S. official propagandists would need to be unduly concerned about the reaction of this particular audience on this issue. However, there were clearly stated limits to the British Government's support for U.S. bombing: just as the British public disapproved of North Vietnamese civilian casualties, so too did the Government. This meant that any change in U.S. bombing targets which might involve the civilian population—and any other target changes which might also make a political settlement harder to reach (such as the mid-1966 Hanoi/Haiphong bombings)—could be expected to displease the British Government—a potential problem which the U.S. Administration had been made aware of from the beginning of escalation by the British Government itself. . . .

France, 1965–1966

The French attitude—governmental, press and public—to U.S. involvement in Vietnam, expressed most forcefully and unambiguously in President [Charles] de Gaulle's pronouncements, was diametrically opposed to that of the British Government's and early press and public's attitude. From 1965 to 1968, until President Johnson's announcement on a bombing cut-back, French President de Gaulle and the French press criticized U.S. involvement in Vietnam. Thus analysis of the French perspective on the war and their reception of U.S. propaganda is comparatively straightforward (unlike the U.K. and West Germany).

De Gaulle's position was based mainly on his assessment of the origins and likely outcome of the conflict (a civil war which would end in defeat for the U.S.); on past French experience in the First Indochina War fighting, and being defeated by, the Vietminh (Vietnamese communists led by Ho Chi Minh, now leader of North Vietnam); on the current war's possible role as a catalyst for a larger conflict in Asia; on his belief that all of Southeast Asia should be neutralized; on his general desire to exert France's independence from U.S. leadership of the Western bloc; and on his wish for a degree of independence from the lingering exigencies of the Cold War—which required better relations with the Eastern bloc . . . There was thus a mixture of domestic and international factors, both historical and current, built into de Gaulle's assessment of the war and U.S. involvement.

Perceiving the conflict as a civil war, provoked by South Vietnam's repressive government and lack of political freedom, de Gaulle discounted the military methods used first to try and quell the unrest in South Vietnam and then subsequently to settle the conflict, on the grounds that political problems could not be solved militarily. And he held the U.S. responsible for escalating the war, propping up the South Vietnamese Government (and so averting its collapse), prolonging the conflict, and thereby preventing a political settlement between North and South Vietnam. For the perceptual framework in which de Gaulle viewed Vietnam was the Algerian Civil War, not the Munich and Second World War of U.S. official propaganda. Thus, President de Gaulle's views on the war—apart from the possibility of a wider conflagration, for which he held the U.S. primarily responsible—were totally at odds with the U.S. Administration's assessments of the conflict and its chances of success . . .

These views, and de Gaulle's habit of airing them privately, but more importantly publicly, were profoundly unwelcome to an Administration which portrayed the war as a crusade for freedom against future communist tyranny, and also perceived the pursuit of the war as a vital manifestation of America's general reliability as an ally. So the Administration was hardly likely to see itself (as others saw it) as merely France's successor in a now quasi-colonial venture. Not unnaturally, Administration officials perceived the current French official and public attitudes to be primarily a product of their previous defeat in Indochina and their resentment over being replaced by the U.S. . . .

Although the press sometimes opined that de Gaulle's criticisms of the U.S. in Vietnam were a little too one-sided—as for instance on the occasion of his Phnom Penh speech on the war in September 1966 when he stated that the U.S. should unilaterally withdraw its troops and stop the bombing—in the main his general foreign policy stance and views on the Vietnam War and the U.S. role were supported by both press and public in France. Thus there was no real danger for de Gaulle of political or public dissension or embarrassment over the official attitude to either U.S. policies or propaganda, as there was in Britain where the potential already existed for the government, its Official Parliamentary opposition, its own Parliamentary Party, and the public to pull in different directions over governmental support for America in Vietnam. For though the British Government might voice careful disapproval of particular U.S. policies—and be embarrassed by them . . . it nevertheless couched such disapproval within a general framework of support for U.S. objectives in Vietnam. De Gaulle, however, could condemn U.S. policies and actions . . . and blame the U.S. entirely for escalating the war, and know that he spoke not only for himself but also for other political parties, the French public, and with the approval of the press . . .

The diplomatic consequence of de Gaulle's (and other officials') statements on Vietnam, particularly after his Phnom Penh speech, was that both the U.S. Administration and the South Vietnamese Government regarded the French position as too biased to be of assistance to them—indeed, diplomatic relations between the French and South Vietnamese governments had ceased in June 1965 on the initiative of the latter due to the French attitude to Saigon and the war. However, while rendering France unacceptable to one side in the conflict, de Gaulle's stance was progressively more appreciated by the North Vietnamese, and thus French officials were well-placed to participate in the continuing saga of peace moves and counter-moves that lasted throughout the war . . . For though the U.S. Administration was displeased by the French attitude and high-level contact was frequently strained, nevertheless a significant degree of contact was maintained between the two governments at lower levels, particularly between the various departments of the Quai and the U.S. embassy.

On occasions these contacts—leaving aside the thorny issue of the peace moves—were of considerable use to the Americans, yielding information from a number of sources, such as the French contact with the North Vietnamese representative in Paris, Mai Van Bo, or the French Ambassadors to China and the Soviet Union. This information added to the general picture of the North Vietnamese and their allies, but sometimes French officials also attempted to help the Americans through their access to the North Vietnamese, as in the case of the latter's threat in December 1965 to put U.S. prisoners of war on trial and execute them. The Quai d'Orsay (French Foreign Office) official in charge of Asian Affairs, Etienne Manac'h, protested to Mai Van Bo on humanitarian grounds, pointing out that "world public opinion would consider it inadmissible to execute prisoners of war under such circumstances," a message that Bo agreed to transmit to Hanoi "immediately" (Embtel 3486 [Paris] McBride to Secretary of State, 18 December 1965, . . . LBJ Library). The threatened trials never took place, and whilst the precise effect of the French intervention cannot be ascertained, the fact is that the North Vietnamese valued the increasingly friendly contact with the French Government . . . and at the very least the French protest would have added to the weight of condemnation of the proposed trials.

Thus, though the French Government was impervious to U.S. official propaganda on the war's origins and the dangers of monolithic Sino-Soviet communist expansionism, though it consistently opposed U.S. policies in Vietnam and the means used to try and attain its objectives, specifically the bombing raids whether used as a carrot or a stick, still French officials played a useful role. In addition, de Gaulle's assessment of the will and capability of the North Vietnamese, as opposed to the inherent and fatal political and social weakness of the South Vietnamese regime(s), proved to be far more accurate than the analyses of the U.S. and its other European supporters. Unfortunately the demands of U.S. global and regional policy, and the predilections of some of Johnson's advisers, determined that French expertise and advice on this issue would be ignored in favour of more optimistic assessments of the war's outcome and support from more compliant European allies, until the shock of the Tet Offensive in 1968, when the Administration was finally forced to confront the spectre of a never-ending and continuously escalating war of attrition, which three years of continual bombing and ground combat had failed to stave off. . . .

European Media to 1967

As stated earlier, the U.S. Administration's propaganda campaign was waged with three broad goals in mind: to persuade its audiences to perceive the war as the Administration wished it to be perceived; to convince its audiences of the necessity and importance of the war; and to persuade its audiences that the Administration's intentions were peaceful, with force used only as a last resort. . . .

For a number of reasons Administration planning and knowledge is especially important in relation to the early stages and subsequent escalation of the war.

Firstly, from the Administration's point of view this was a crucial stage in the conflict itself. In only three months [in 1965] the Administration had switched from the previous policy of limited involvement with American advisers, to air raids, and then to the dispatch of ground troops, even though in a defensive role. . . .

. . . From the point of view of assessing the Administration's propaganda campaign, recapping briefly on the Administration's knowledge and planning in the early stages of the war will show the extent to which the Administration privately realized what lay ahead, that is, the massive growth of the conflict with its attendant casualties. And having recalled the Administration's private perceptions of the future course of the war it then becomes possible to compare these perceptions with the Administration's view of the conflict contained in official statements and speeches disseminated through the media, and to determine the accuracy and veracity of Administration statements.

As *The Pentagon Papers* demonstrate, Administration planning in the initial stages of the war was detailed, moved rapidly from a defensive to an offensive strategy based on General [William] Westmoreland's search-and-destroy tactics, and focused on the kill ratio as a means to winning this war of attrition . . . The Administration's troop and casualty projections also rose rapidly and as early as November 1965 Defense Secretary McNamara was recommending that by the end of 1966 there should be almost 400,000 troops in South Vietnam, but at the same time he warned the President that this level of deployment "will not guarantee success" and that there was an even chance that the war would be stalemated at "an even higher level" (Sheehan et al., 1971: 466). And as the troop figures rocketed, so naturally did those for casualties: by November 1965 McNamara estimated that "U.S. killed-in-action can be expected to reach 1,000 a month"—compared with his recommendation to the president a mere three months earlier in July that "U.S. killed-in-action might be in the vicinity of 500 a month by the end of the year" (Sheehan et al., 1971: 464–6).

The results of the Administration's propaganda policy will now be examined, concentrating on media coverage (primarily press coverage in the first three years of the conflict) of some particularly important incidents and issues following escalation of the war. . . .

. . . Not surprisingly, the planning of the Administration often bore little resemblance to press coverage of these issues, for in Washington the press was dependent on official briefings, on private contacts in the Administration and other officials' views, and on what it could piece together from any other relevant sources (in South Vietnam, however, there were not only official sources, but there was also the possibility of eye-witness accounts of the war and events in Saigon—which might contradict the official version).

Thus, when McNamara and Johnson were contemplating sending 400,000 troops to Vietnam, the press was wondering whether the figure might reach 200,000, at a time when there were still 'only' 184,000 troops there (Sheehan et al., 1971:466). And this discrepancy was due to the Administration's desire to keep publicity about its war policies to a minimum, and thereby to avoid public disquiet about U.S. involvement in a conflict which had already assumed vastly greater proportions and intensity than only a few months previously. And of course this publicity embargo also covered the unwelcome discovery that the enemy was matching U.S. troop deployments, which meant that the U.S. commitment—given the opposing views of the U.S. and the Vietcong/North Vietnam, and South Vietnam's weakness—was open-ended in a war in which "winning" would be hard to determine, as the Administration knew.

This, however, was not a conclusion which the Administration wanted publicized, for it had rejected from the beginning the other course open to it, that of openly declaring war, seeking a Congressional Declaration, and publicly rallying the nation in support of its objectives. So instead the Administration tried to fight what quickly became a major war with minimal information, hoping that as the conflict dragged on the public would support an ill-understood and vicious war for which it had not been prepared. And when the media speculated about the war more than the Administration wished, or provided estimates closer to the truth than the latter wished—thereby enabling the general public to gain a more accurate (usually less optimistic) view of the war—then the Administration promptly rounded on the U.S. press, accusing it of hostile and inaccurate news coverage, as did the British and West German Governments with their media.

On the other hand, eager press speculation about vague Administration hints about peace moves (however unlikely) *was* encouraged at particular junctures—and discouraged at others: what top Administration officials wanted from the press was the dissemination of the official line on the war—whatever it was and however contradictory the statements—and the portrayal of the war in the type of black and white terms in which the Second World War could be perceived and portrayed. The irony was that even those journalists who agreed wholeheartedly with the U.S. involvement in Vietnam still criticized the Administration's public relations campaign for its ineptitude and paucity of information (*Daily Telegraph*, 10 June 1965), and for its "misleading" public stance on peace talks ([Joseph] Alsop in the *New York Herald Tribune*, 20–21 November 1965).

Considering the number of times that the Administration was caught out by its own information policy—that is, when its war policies or current events directly contradicted official statements, or when the past intruded into the present and demonstrated how economical with "details" the Administration had been—the Administration was given the benefit of the doubt for a considerable length of time. For most press criticism in the U.S., U.K. and West Germany was initially directed at the results of U.S. war methods and the difficulties engendered by U.S. official propaganda. *The Guardian*'s leader writer in Britain questioned U.S. involvement from early 1965 on legal, political and moral grounds, while the *Observer* fretted about the war's deleterious impact on international relations, considering it to be an obstacle to the growing *détente* between East and West. But most other mainstream newspapers in the UK, and those in West Germany (France was obviously the exception from the beginning), supported the U.S. with much the same justifications that U.S. official propaganda put forward, with the added elements that the U.S. had never lost a war (so victory was expected) and was still associated with "just" causes.

Nevertheless journalists still reported what they saw in the field in South Vietnam, and Washington correspondents reported official Administration statements and private views, and often these reports alone were enough to cast doubts on the Administration's credibility, despite the overall agreement with the Administration's objectives. Because the root cause of the Administration's "credibility gap" lay in its own information policies: the "gap" was merely exposed by the press, often inadvertently, not created by them.

This issue of credibility affected the Administration in several ways. Firstly there was the straightforward issue of "truth"-telling or—to remove the element of subjective perception contained in the word "truth"—whether and to what degree the Administration's version of events, current and past, accorded with the actual events being reported, by participants or eye-witnesses. Such an issue could be determined on a reasonably factual basis, even though interpretations of the events in question could still differ.

For instance, the Administration's stance on peace talks was that the U.S. was willing to discuss this issue at any time and any place with the communists, but the latter unfortunately refused to contemplate such discussion. The President's speeches on peace were invariably welcomed enthusiastically by the press and public and were believed for quite some time; thus the onus for the lack of talks was placed entirely on the intransigence of the communists. However, in November 1965 it became known through the press (in fact [UN Secretary General] U Thant had hinted of this even earlier in the year, but the issue was not taken up then) that the U.S. had turned down an opportunity to discuss the war with Hanoi in late 1964. And in view of the Administration's previous trumpeting of the communist unwillingness to talk, this revelation caused a storm of press protest. In a stinging editorial *The New York Times* commented.

> . . . Secretary Rusk, according to Mr. [State Department Spokesman Robert] McCloskey has a "sensitive antenna" and he would have known—or sensed—when North Vietnam was really prepared for peace talks. This comment reminds one of the ancient Roman practice of draw-

> ing auspices from the flight or entrails of birds. It would be a shuddering thought that the fate of nations and of thousands of young Americans depended on Dean Rusk's antenna. Yet this is what Mr. McCloskey indicated. . . .

Thus this particular episode dealt a blow not only to the credibility of the Administration's stance on peace talks—having not only rejected an offer, but also according to Alsop having made its offer(s) purely for public consumption, that is, purely for propaganda purposes in popular terms—but also undermined its general credibility, having been firstly "economical" with its facts about the communists refusing to talk and then having to admit to the original allegation that an offer was turned down. This was a syndrome that had already happened in the past on an equally important issue: the tardy public admission in June 1965 of a change in troop role (secretly authorized in April) from defensive to offensive, that is, the admission of a ground war in Asia. And the difficulty for the Administration lay in the fact that whether or not its original peace offer(s) were just "propaganda", it was now more than ever imperative that it continue to make such offers in order to avoid being labelled more widely as "mere propagandists" and so further eroding its support among the public. And this was a trap that the Administration had created for itself in originally whetting its audiences' appetite for peace, whilst having—according to *The Pentagon Papers*—no intention of negotiating on terms that were less than a North Vietnamese surrender, which the Administration also knew was highly unlikely.

Similarly, when the U.S. bombed the Hanoi area in December 1966, Administration spokesmen categorically denied that there were civilian casualties. However, due to the presence of the Managing Director of the *New York Times* (Harrison Salisbury) in Hanoi at the same time as the bombing raids, these official U.S. statements were themselves comprehensively and damagingly contradicted—on a matter of fact, not interpretation. Again the Administration's credibility was damaged, and the damage was compounded in the way in which spokesmen first denied the charge and then were forced to admit it. . . .

. . . "British papers were skeptical of U.S. explanations" and the reports quoted in it show that this press skepticism covered the spectrum of stances on Vietnam. Reactions ranged from the *Daily Telegraph* which usually supported the U.S. and so fairly mildly noted the unavoidability of "incidental damage to civilian life and property"; through the *Observer*'s complaints about the "credibility gap" reaching its "peak"; to the much less surprising comments of the "hypercritical" *Guardian*, which perceptively judged that the raids would ". . . insure that the truces [holiday truces] do not blossom into any negotiations except on Washington's terms." . . . Adverse French press comment was of course expected, but fortunately "fell off after an early spate of skeptical or sarcastic comment on U.S. statements." But again the comment was perceptive, this time focusing on the contradictory explanations that could emanate from Washington and Saigon, thereby revealing more of the Administration's planning than it wanted to be made public:

> Today's pro-Gaullist *Paris-Jour* said: 'In Europe, the "explanations" by the military command in Saigon—especially in regard to North Vietnamese rockets falling'on Hanoi, 'have convinced nobody'—all the more so since the U.S. military in Saigon had earlier said the bombardment of Hanoi 'was a decision which they had at last obtained from President Johnson.' . . .

By the end of December, after Harrison Salisbury's articles had appeared in the *New York Times* detailing civilian damage and casualties, the Administration faced another barrage of criticism. . . .

Although it subsequently became known that some of Salisbury's information about the damage and casualties had come from communist sources—which he had failed to disclose—the fact remained that the Administration handled the whole episode badly on a number of counts. Firstly, the impression had been given in official briefings that very little damage or civilian casualties occurred due to the precision bombing only of military targets, thus also endeavoring to give the impression of a clean, clinical war—something which official language also tried to reinforce. Secondly, the Administration then flatly denied the charges of U.S. involvement in any damage and casualties, and then tried to attribute this to the communists' own rockets. And thirdly, official spokesmen were then forced to admit that such damage had occurred as a result of U.S. bombing. So although Salisbury's reports contained some communist propaganda, the administration was hardly in a position to complain about this, having itself disseminated an inaccurate picture, from the beginning, of the effects of U.S. bombing—in other words, presenting a biased view. For though the Administration was not deliberately targeting civilian areas and most newspapers recognized this, what mattered was the official denial of any such damage followed by the tardy admission that this sort of damage was in fact virtually inevitable. . . .

These are instances in which the Administration's general reputation for disseminating accurate accounts of events was publicly eroded, but there was also another way in which the Administration's credibility was slowly impaired and this concerned the progress—or lack of it—in the war. For the continuous escalation of the war in intensity and carnage cast doubt on the ability of the U.S. to do the job it had set out to do at a cost that was acceptable, not only in domestic political terms, but also in terms of world opinion. The difficulty that the U.S. administration faced was that these two sets of demands, internal public opinion and external opinion, were not easily reconcilable while the U.S. was trying to fight and win the war.

Obviously, U.S. public opinion was primarily concerned about U.S. war casualties and the financial strain of the war, and this resulted in pressure on the Administration to show some sort of "progress" in order to justify these human and financial costs fighting a confusing war. Yet, as mentioned previously, this was a difficult task for U.S. propaganda in a war with no front lines and a frequently elusive enemy: thus the kill-ratio was the statistic used for the combatants, and then there were the statistics for the pacification effort, and aid generally to South Vietnam—all designed to measure the war and then publicized to show that the U.S. was making "progress."...

... The Administration did not have unlimited time to fight a vicious war of attrition, as the President and his top advisers knew. Added to the pressure to demonstrate progress for domestic opinion was the pressure from the President's military advisers to continually escalate and intensify the war, both to try and break the stalemate and achieve victory, and to minimize U.S. casualties. And the President responded to this pressure because there was little alternative but withdrawal. Moreover the U.S. public responded favourably to the implementation of clear-cut Administration policies—whether these involved an escalation in bombing or the announcement of a peace move.... And so the mainstream U.S. public continued to support the war (though this support was slowly eroding) until time ran out after the Tet Offensive in 1968—it was the anti-war protesters who early on objected to the destruction and the war itself.

World opinion, however, was less concerned with the rise in U.S. casualties, or the need to minimize them by using air-strikes for instance, than with the cost of the war in terms of the carnage in South and North Vietnam, and the war's impact on international relations—particularly the possibility of a wider conflagration. Therefore escalation was queried both on the grounds of the sheer scale of the destruction and that peace would be harder to achieve.

The Administration was thus in a cleft stick, needing to escalate to try and attain its objectives, and in order to retain domestic support (given that its brand of peace moves was unlikely to be successful), but in doing so progressively alienating foreign public opinion, including the media—which reported the carnage. For the European media would publish articles which the U.S. press were apparently chary of publishing as "unsuitable for American readers" (Gellhorn, 1986: 254). Thus Martha Gellhorn's series of articles in September 1966 appeared in *The Guardian.* Focusing on the U.S. campaign to win "Hearts and Minds" in South Vietnam, they carried descriptions of the effects of U.S. war methods on the population in South Vietnam—including the results of napalm and the refugee camps created—war methods which inherently defeated the drive to win over the people:

> We are not maniacs or monsters; but our planes range the sky all day and all night and our artillery is lavish and we have much more deadly stuff to kill with. The people are there on the ground, sometimes destroyed by accident, sometimes destroyed because the Vietcong are reported to be among them. This is indeed a new kind of war, as the [U.S.] indoctrination lecture stated, and we had better find a new way to fight it. Hearts and minds, after all, live in bodies. (*The Guardian*, 12 September 1966: "A New Kind of War")

For all that the articles were too much for the U.S. market, and that *The Guardian*'s editor considered that Gellhorn's articles "brought home, more effectively than anything I had read until then, the horror and the human cost of the war" (Hetherington, 1981: 228), in later years Gellhorn herself remarked that her articles on Vietnam "are a model of self-censorship" but that "to be heard at all, I had to suppress half of what I knew and gentle the rest" (Gellhorn, 1986: 254). It seems therefore, that even what was then taken to be (too) robust reporting of the war's carnage fell well short of depicting reality.

Nevertheless these articles, however "gentle", came at a time when the Administration could ill afford reports of the war's costs, for at the end of June 1966 the war had been escalated dramatically by the bombing of North Vietnam's petroleum, oil and lubricants (P.O.L.) depots near Hanoi and Haiphong, in an effort to cripple North Vietnam's continuing ability to wage war . . . The raids were ultimately unsuccessful militarily, as the CIA had warned they would be, in that although 76 per cent of North Vietnam's bulk storage capacity was eliminated, sufficient supplies remained, supplemented by imports to meet North Vietnam's requirements, as had become apparent at the end of that summer; so infiltration continued and North Vietnam kept up the fight (Gravel, 1971, vol. IV: 29). Furthermore, the effect of the raids on America's allied government supporters was to increase the difficulties they already faced by mid-1966 in continuing to back U.S. involvement, due to a growing gap between governmental and general public sympathies.

Although a special effort had been made to enlist U.K. Prime Minister Wilson's support for the raids, this failed and Wilson felt obliged to publicly dissociate the British Government from these bombings . . .

The overall mood in Europe following the raids was noted in USIA's [U.S. Information Agency's] media round-up: "Press reports of a widespread wave of indignation, dramatized by anti-US demonstrations in Europe, India, and Japan, were reprinted all over the world.". . . In addition, Administration optimism following the air raids was also discounted: French writers were reported to be skeptical about North Vietnam's supposed lack of expectation of a military victory combined with its "war weariness", attributing this official optimism to "upcoming Congressional elections". . .

Thus these raids, having firstly severely embarrassed European allied governments and sparked off demonstrations, finally resulted in a deleterious sharpening of the focus on U.S. war methods and aims.

The Tet Offensive, 1968: Media Coverage

The final blow as far as the Administration's credibility was concerned came in late 1967, when the Administration launched a campaign which had as one of its purposes the intention to demonstrate "progress" in the war, for which General Westmoreland was required, as Hammond notes:

> Although the purpose of the meeting was supposedly to discuss how the United States could achieve maximum progress during the next six months, there appears to have been little doubt in military circles that the general [Westmoreland] was participating in a major public relations initiative. His presence in Washington created opportunities not only to promote the theme of progress in the war but also to attack critics of the Administration's war policies and to bolster the president's sagging standing in the polls. (Hammond, 1988: 333) . . .

A West German newspaper . . . observed that Johnson "had created the impression that the end of the tunnel is in sight. . .If he is able to maintain that impression, Johnson may win in the end, in the elections as well as in Viet-Nam, for Hanoi's perseverance is inspired by the idea that domestic considerations will compel the U.S. to give in sooner or later" . . . Unfortunately for the Administration, rather than the end of the tunnel being in sight, what lay just round the corner was the Tet Offensive, which began just two months after this officially inaugurated bout of optimism....

From the beginning of the offensive [European] correspondents' reports suggested that the communists' aims were to gain political and psychological ground, rather than a military victory, and they noted that the mere mounting of the offensive constituted a rebuttal of U.S. propaganda, as "conservative" *Figaro* of Paris pointed out:

> "American positions are not endangered . . . This was not General Giap's aim. He aims at two objectives, both of an essentially political nature. On the domestic level, the Viet Cong has just won an enormous victory.
>
> "It has demonstrated to the Vietnamese population that it is capable of striking where and when it wants to. It ridicules the Saigon government and its army. It tightens its hold, at Saigon's expense, on a civilian population not necessarily friendly but filled with respect, fear and admiration . . .
>
> "Giap's second objective was evidently the American home front. His message is clear . . . 'We are stronger than ever.' The military authorities and President Johnson will find it rather difficult to demonstrate the contrary." (Worldwide Treatment of Current Issues, 31 January 1968: 4) . . .

. . . on 2 February the reports that USIA included in its summary began: 'As correspondents' reports and shocking pictures brought home the "dreadful toll" of the street fighting in South Vietnamese cities, press commentators assessed the Viet Cong attacks as designed to win a political and psychological victory. Most thought they had succeeded, at least in part.'. . .

The summing-up of the offensive, beginning on 5 February, carried a dual message for the Administration. On the one hand, as the USIA media summary noted: "Influential British papers this morning emphasized that the people of South Viet-Nam did not rise to support the Viet Cong as liberators, but frightened civilians might become more submissive to Communist pressures as a result of the audacious attacks." And on the other hand, the same USIA report stated: "Media in various countries saw the Viet Cong onslaught in the supposedly safe areas of South Viet-Nam as bringing into serious question the official U.S. position that the allied forces had been making "slow but steady progress."...

> "For the first time since the beginning of the war in Viet-Nam, the ability of the American generals is being criticized in the U.S. Another consequence of the Viet Cong offensive is that the Saigon government is openly accused of indifference. And serious doubts are voiced regarding the possibility of pacifying South Viet-Nam, as much by the press as by Congressional circles and public opinion.
>
> "Discontent is shaping up, and even if it is not shared by the White House, some of Johnson's advisers are ready to admit that it is not without foundation . . . (*France-Soir* report cited in Worldwide Treatment of Current Issues, 7 February 1968: 3) . . .

Thus most of the Administration's propaganda arguments were dismissed in these media observations. And most importantly, USIA's summary of media reaction outside the U.S. shows that apart from some initial "sensational newsplay" on the guerrilla attack on the U.S. embassy in Saigon (Worldwide Treatment of Current Issues, 31 January 1968: 1), much of the subsequent commentary focused on the significance of the offensive for both sides, with even the carnage being set in this broader context. Thus the allegations made against the U.S. press that it sensationalized the Tet Offensive, exaggerating the horror, disseminating the impression of a U.S. military defeat, and thereby creating a North Vietnamese/Viet Cong psychological and political victory, do not appear to apply to the European media. The latter quite rightly set the attacks within the context of U.S. Administration claims of progress in the war and pacification and saw the offensive as a rebuttal to these claims, and therefore a psychological and political setback; but equally the communists were seen to have suffered a setback in the lack of an uprising in the South. Thus the defeat for the U.S. focused on the hollowness of its claims . . .

As the war lengthened and intensified, the problems that U.S. propaganda had to cope with, and by extension its allies' propaganda, changed and multiplied. As noted previously . . . the initial task was to fix in the audiences' minds the justice of aiding South Vietnam militarily by blaming North Vietnam entirely for the turmoil in the South, with the concomitant need for the bombing campaign and the subsequent escalation of the war in the air and on the ground. This goal was mostly achieved (the main exception being French reaction), and was aided in the first few months of the war by press dissemination of the view that the Administration sincerely desired peace, and that therefore it was escalating reluctantly because of communist intransigence over negotiations. However, the accuracy of this picture was challenged and gradually modified during the years of public revelations about a number of important issues and events in the war, such as the nature of South Vietnamese "democracy" and "freedom"; the Administration's attitude to various peace moves during the war, and revelations about its past response, provoking doubts abut the sincerity of "peace" statements; and the confusion engendered by the nature of, and progress in, the war and the destruction caused by methods of fighting it.

The net result of the above factors was to slowly erode the Administration's credibility, resulting in even more debate on its statements on virtually all aspects of the war. And this diminution in Administration credibility and strength of its position . . . was a bonus for the North Vietnamese and Vietcong, for though the latter's credibility and the strength of their case did not necessarily increase to the degree that the Administration's diminished, nevertheless it did become harder to dismiss the North Vietnamese/Vietcong case summarily, as had often happened earlier in the war. And the shifts that occurred in public perceptions of the Administration were accompanied by an erosion of support for the U.S. venture and a steady strengthening of the desire for a U.S. withdrawal. Thus the public climate in which U.S. propagandists and allied governments operated became increasingly more unfavorable . . .

United Kingdom Government Reaction

To the North Vietnamese, by December 1965 the British Government was too closely aligned with the U.S. to be able to act as a mediator . . . In diplomatic terms this meant that the British Government could act neither formally, in its role as Co-Chairman of the Geneva Conference, nor informally as one of the many nations which desired an end to hostilities, with any hope of success. Also, according to North Vietnamese Prime Minister Pham Van Dong, speaking in December 1965, any country desiring to mediate would first have to denounce U.S. aggression (*Evening Standard*, 13 December 1965). But the British Government's policy was based on the assumption that public criticism—let alone denunciation—of U.S. actions would immediately diminish any influence that it could exert on U.S. policy, an eventuality it desired to avoid. There seemed little chance therefore that the British Government would ever be in a position to satisfy the North Vietnamese requirement. . . .

For much of the first year of the war, the saving grace for the British Government, as for the Administration, was that so often the North Vietnamese Government publicly rejected negotiation proposals. . . . So while the North Vietnamese and Vietcong (and Chinese) were perceived as opposed to negotiations, the fact that the British Government was in the process of rendering itself unable to mediate the conflict was obscured, and in these circumstances British support for U.S. policy had even been endorsed in a *Guardian* editorial in late September 1965 . . .

However, as doubts grew about the sincerity of the Administration's approach to peace moves, and as the war continued to escalate, the British Government's policy of refraining from criticizing the U.S., in order to try and exercise some influence over U.S. policy, was itself being criticized by June 1966—even before the intensification presaged by the P.O.L. bombings. In a reversal of its September evaluation of the Government's performance, *The Guardian* stated that the Prime Minister should "speak out" against U.S. policy, out of "loyalty to the alliance, and his concern for the wellbeing of its leading member", and concluded: "There is no virtue in cheering on a friend marching blindly into a swamp" (*The Guardian*, 1 June 1966: "Plunging Ahead in Vietnam"). In fact, at that very moment President Johnson was privately endeavoring to persuade Wilson to support him in a giant step into the swamp—the P.O.L. bombings in Hanoi and Haiphong. . . .

The P.O.L. bombings in the summer of 1966 were a prime example of one of these important junctures, with repercussions not only for the Administration's propaganda effort, but also for the U.S.-U.K. relationship. At first sight the clear, detailed, advance warning given by Prime Minister Wilson to the President meant that the Administration knew the British Government would dissociate from the P.O.L. bombings, and on what grounds. Thus the Administration's irritated reaction—noted publicly in the press—appears on the surface to be unwarranted, given that advance warning. However, there is a telegram from President Johnson to Prime Minster Wilson, classified "Top Secret", which goes some way to explaining the President's and his top officials' "deep chagrin" over the British dissociation, and the subsequent growth in Johnson's apparent distrust of Wilson. . .

This telegram, dated 14 June 1966 and carrying the further handling instruction to the U.S. embassy of EXDIS (Exclusive Distribution), thus indicating the special sensitivity of the message, discussed both Vietnam and Wilson's upcoming visit to Washington. On the former, after explaining the reasons for the proposed bombing raids and noting Rusk's "private talk" with Wilson about "the problem of POL in Haiphong and Hanoi", President Johnson expressed the hope that Wilson would be able "to maintain solidarity with us despite what you said in the House of Commons about Haiphong and Hanoi". Stressing that the mooted P.O.L. attacks were not "an air assault on civilian centers but a specific attack on POL installations with a direct relevance to the fighting in the South", Johnson then sharply attacked the British position of non-combat support for the U.S. from the angle of SEATO obligations:

> I hope that you can give further thought to your own interests and commitments in Southeast Asia under the SEATO Treaty. Dean [Rusk, Secretary of State] tells me that, in his talk with you and your colleagues, several references were made to the "revival of SEATO." South Vietnam and five signatories of SEATO are not talking about a revival but are committing troops to repel an armed attack from the north. Nor do I believe that your role as co-chairman [of the 1954 Geneva Conference] means that Britain should stand aside; the other co-chairman [the Soviet Union] is furnishing large quantities of sophisticated arms and other assistance to North Viet Nam and is, therefore, an active partner in the effort to take over South Viet Nam by force. (Cable, President Johnson to Prime Minister Wilson, 14 June 1966, "Wilson Visit", National Security Files of Walt W. Rostow, . . . LBJ Library; square brackets added) . . .

When the P.O.L. storage depots were bombed Wilson reacted swiftly, issuing a statement which firmly dissociated the Government from these attacks, expressed general support for the U.S. assistance for South Vietnam and U.S. proposals for unconditional negotiations, and blamed North Vietnam for the lack of negotiations and the continued fighting (*The Guardian*, 30 June 1966: 'Attacks "Noted with Regret" - Premier'). Thus several of the elements requested by the Administration did appear in Wilson's statement, but, importantly, he also referred to the location of the targets and "populated areas" . . .

The effects of the dissociation, and this particular reference, on the Administration were summed up by Henry Brandon, Associate Editor of the *Sunday Times* and a Washington columnist noted for his sources in the Administration, which ensured a considerable degree of accuracy in his articles. Brandon's article tended to confirm the suspicion voiced in other press articles that relations between the two allies would be more difficult after the British dissociation. He noted the Administration's surprise at the speed of Wilson's dissociation, and concern over his mention of ' "targets touching on the populated areas of Hanoi and Haiphong" when even the Russians, it is pointed out with slight irritation, referred only to targets on the "outskirts" '. . . .

. . . For although Wilson's visit to Washington on 29 July appeared to contradict predictions that the Prime Minister's reception would be less than warm—in fact the President toasted Wilson in hugely flattering terms despite having once more been refused the token British force that he had long desired—and though Wilson's memoirs record the visit as untroubled by any difficulties (Wilson, 1971: 262–5), given Lyndon Johnson's views on loyalty—that it should be absolute—the consequences of Wilson's dissociation were always likely to be considerable. Thus the public appearance of White House "charitable equanimity" and the warm reception given to Wilson were ultimately misleading, and the dissociation could be expected not only to affect relations between the two leaders, but also to further affect the reception accorded by the Administration to British peace initiatives—a reception which had been erratic at the best of times, and was often unenthusiastic. . . .

. . . Though the British Government refrained from publicly dissociating again from U.S. policy, despite the almost constant escalation and intensification of the war, what little chance the Government had of mediating—and it was probably only ever a slender chance—vanished with the dissociation. . . .

The demise of its most serious attempt to arrange negotiations [in early 1967], and the subsequent strain on the Anglo-American relationship, meant that the Wilson government was thereafter unable to mute criticism of its policy of support for the U.S. by hinting at secret peace moves, or indeed by endeavoring to undertake them. And thus the continuing, and apparently inevitable (given the lengthy list of failed peace attempts) escalation of the war, accompanied by increased dissatisfaction with government policy and growing violence at demonstrations and marches, posed a problem that the government was now poorly placed to counteract while it continued to support U.S. policy in Vietnam. Though the criticism and violence in the U.K. did not pose a political danger to the government, it was an embarrassment which could only strengthen, for included in it was a factor over which the British Government had no control, that is, U.S. war policy (the riots and demonstrations in Europe at this time incorporated more than just anger over Vietnam, but the latter was undoubtedly a cause of unrest, as well as a symbol of dissatisfaction with other aspects of "the system").

The government soon had a taste of what was to come in October 1967, when there was a weekend of riots in Europe, including a violent demonstration in London in which the U.S. embassy was attacked. These were quickly followed by the 1968 riots, in March and October in Britain, and in France the most famous of all the riots in May. Increasingly there appeared a gulf between government policy on Vietnam and public sentiment, expressed not only in these riots but also through opinion polls, in which the general, non-rioting public, while disliking the violent anti-war demonstrations and student riots, nevertheless still disagreed with the main thrust of official policy. Some relief was provided with Johnson's post-Tet announcement in March 1968 that he was henceforth seeking peace and not standing for re-election, but still the war ground on while the negotiators argued—and the demonstrations also continued with Vietnam as a theme. . . .

So by 1968 the British Government had failed to achieve anything of note concerning Vietnam itself with its policy of support for the Administration, being neither able to influence U.S. policy nor mediate a settlement. However, though its policy was a failure on those terms the government had managed to retain U.S. support for its domestic policies and had avoided having to provide a more concrete manifestation of its support in the shape of troops, despite considerable U.S. pressure. The problem for the government was that whilst the riots in Britain expressed dissatisfaction with more than just the Vietnam War, there was still a considerable, vocal, and active opposition that was centered solely on the war, and the government's policy was clearly unable to damp down this sentiment, and was more likely to fuel it. But even if the government had dissociated completely from the Administration and condemned the latter's policies in Vietnam, it is highly unlikely that the demonstrations would have stopped as long as the war itself dragged on. For just as the war was only one factor in some of the riots, so British Government policy was only one element in these protests against Vietnam, in which the fact of the war itself played a larger part—both as a particularly devastating war and as a manifestation of a conflict between a small Third World nation and the technological (and to some, imperialist) giant of the West.

French Government Reaction

Although de Gaulle's vocal, increasingly anti-American and pro-North Vietnam stance circumscribed the role that France played during the first three years of the war—in tune with his belief that until the U.S. realized it could not win the war militarily, and opted for a diplomatic solution, there was no role that France *could* usefully, or successfully undertake (see extract from de Gaulle's Phnom Penh speech in Lacouture, 1992: 404–5)—unlike the British Government such public diplomatic inaction (though it was accompanied by de Gaulle's denunciations) was no handicap to the French Government . . . For this policy also underlined France's independence from the U.S. (given added weight by France's withdrawal from NATO's military wing in July 1966), as well as insulating the former both from the consequences of yet another divisive war, and from the constant pressure exerted by the latter on other allies to extend at least diplomatic and material support, if troops were not to be forthcoming. And where America's other allies were cajoled or hectored into offering this support—and taken to task if they did not offer enough (see below)—de Gaulle early on dismissed the entire affray with the grand observation at a ministerial meeting: "We are not disposed to accompany the Americans into every adventure that they think fit to throw themselves into" (cited in Lacouture, 1992: 403).

De Gaulle's policy also had the added benefit of keeping France clear of the repeated and fruitless mediation attempts which other countries undertook, and which usually ended in recriminations of varying degrees of bitterness. And even though U.S. policy generated disapproval across a wide political spectrum among politicians, the general public, and the media, there was no corresponding pressure on de Gaulle to try and produce a settlement, as there was in Britain. For de Gaulle's analysis of and approach to the problem was mostly accepted, and thus he had no need to discuss or undertake mediation attempts in order to fulfill diplomatic duties, give an impression of purposeful activity, or silence critics, as did the British Prime Minister.

Nevertheless, despite his condemnation of U.S. policies in Vietnam, when de Gaulle was approached for permission to allow one of the most spectacular events opposing American actions in Vietnam to be staged in France, namely the Russell Tribunal on U.S. "war crimes" in Vietnam, he refused. And the grounds on which he refused show clearly the importance he assigned to the nation-state as an entity in global affairs, and the importance of upholding the rights of the nation-state—whatever policies a state chose to pursue, and however such policies were viewed by the French Government when headed by de Gaulle:

> The initiators of the "Russell Tribunal" propose to criticize the Vietnam policy of the United States . . . Quite apart from the fact that the written and spoken word are free in our country, there would be no reason to turn down private individuals, particularly those whose theses on this subject are so close to the official position of the French Republic. But what is at stake here is neither the right to free assembly nor to free speech but the duty—all the more imperative for France as she has taken a position on the basic issue which is known to all—to see to it that no state with which she has relations and which in spite of all differences remains her traditional friend become, on her territory, the object of a procedure which runs counter to general law and international custom . . . (Grosser, 1980: 242)

Thus on this issue the Administration benefited from de Gaulle's belief in the nation-state (a belief that was also apparent in de Gaulle's vision of and attitude towards the European Economic Community) which influenced the expression of his opposition to U.S. policy in Vietnam and the U.S. position as leader of the Western bloc. For though the Russell Tribunal still took place, it was convened in Stockholm, and therefore denied the degree of credibility that being held in France—considering France's background of involvement in Indochina, current political stance and role as a medium power in the world—would have conferred on it. In addition, convening the tribunal in France would have granted it a higher profile and perhaps brought a greater amount of media coverage. So de Gaulle's rebuff prevented France from being embroiled in a profitless exercise that was viewed as an anti-American propaganda spectacle from the beginning, with the Tribunal having already reached its verdict before the proceedings started (for contemporary reportage of the Tribunal, see Worldwide Treatment of Current Issues, 1 May 1967: 3; for differing views of its activities see Caute, 1988: 7–8, 12–13; and Lewy, 1978: 311–13).

However, despite the fact that the French Government's disapproval of the U.S. involvement in Vietnam generated widespread approval in France, the latter did not escape the riots and demonstrations that erupted across Europe, with the Vietnam War as one theme among several others, such as student conditions (also a factor in Britain), the government and education authorities' attitude to students, and what Caute terms "the wider grievance against technocratic authoritarianism" (Caute, 1988: 186; see also 68–71 and 183–209). Paradoxically the worst of the riots in France, in May 1968 and then again in October, took place after President Johnson's March announcement of a bombing cutback coupled with a readiness to negotiate. However, though the demonstrators were obviously unmoved by this development, de Gaulle welcomed it publicly as a genuine move in the direction of peace, even hailing Johnson's decision as "an act of wisdom and political courage" (see Worldwide Treatment of Current Issues, 3 April 1968: 4).

Johnson's speech and de Gaulle's reaction initiated a better relationship between the two leaders concerning Vietnam, which was ultimately an important factor in beginning the peace process in Paris. For though France's friendly relations with Hanoi meant that the French government was well-placed to help in any negotiation process (as Paris Radio was quick to point out; see Worldwide Treatment of Current Issues, 1 April 1968: 5), the French Government's past opposition to the policies of the Johnson Administration and Saigon, coupled with its pro-Hanoi stance, had appeared to vitiate any chance that the French might have had to mediate in the conflict, by becoming unacceptable to the Americans and South Vietnamese—much as the British Government was now unacceptable to the North Vietnamese because of its pro-American stance. For American displeasure with the French Government's attitude had apparently reached further than just top Administration officials, as French officials themselves had been aware, and this discontent could have impacted on American public opinion concerning a site for peace talks:

> When I called on Lucet [Charles Lucet, the new French Ambassador to the U.S.] at his request at Foreign Office this morning, I found him tired and discouraged . . . Lucet said he was forced to conclude that there existed very genuine resentment at French policies in US, and that there was a general distrust of France. He cited recent polls in this connection. He said US opinion did not seem to pinpoint its dissatisfaction with France but that there certainly was an increasingly unfortunate climate. I of course cited French policies on NATO and Vietnam as fundamental reasons for this unhappy attitude which he found in US. (Embtel 1393 [Paris] McBride to State Department, 28 July 1966, . . . LBJ Library; square brackets added) . . .

. . .And where Vietnam was concerned this distrust had been fully reciprocated by the French, right up to President Johnson's post-Tet speech:

> There is in France . . . a new and great wave of violent opposition to our Viet Nam policy . . .
>
> We are seen as the greatest power in the world towering over little people in a little country. The enemy's casualty rate is proof of the cruel power we wield. The enemy's ability to continue to attack after suffering great losses is proof of the honesty and sincerity and the rightness of his desire to expel the alien invader . . .
>
> Europeans are skeptics and cynics. They do not believe we are spending blood and treasure in Viet Nam for an altruistic even abstract reason such as preventing aggression. (Memo, Ernest Goldstein for the President, 23 February 1968, . . . LBJ Library) . . .

In addition to its relationship with North Vietnam, the other point in France's favour was that however poor the public relations between the top echelons of the U.S. and French Governments, as mentioned previously contacts had always continued quietly at the lower governmental levels, and French Government officials, as well as private individuals, had been involved in peace probes between the two sides. With the change in approach by Johnson and de Gaulle it now became feasible for Paris to be chosen as an acceptable compromise site for peace talks after other possible locations had been discarded.

Discussion Questions: European SEATO Allies

1. How did European perspectives differ from American perspectives on the Vietnam War?

2. Why did the British Government support the U.S. in the Vietnam War, but refuse to send troops? Why did Prime Minister Wilson dissociate his Government from the U.S. bombings of petroleum, oil, and lubricants (P.O.L.) depots near Hanoi and Haiphong?

3. Discuss changes in attitudes of the British press—for example, the *Daily Telegraph*, *Times*, and *Guardian*—toward the Vietnam War as time went on. Discuss media coverage of the Tet Offensive.

4. What were the main reasons the French Government opposed U.S. involvement in Vietnam? Was it justified in its opposition to the War?

5. What, if any, support did the U.S. get from its ally France?

6. What primary sources might you use to discover more about perspectives in an European country on the War's escalation during the Johnson Years?

Part Two
The Nixon-Ford Years: Gradual Withdrawal

III. SEATO Allies "Down Under": Australian Gradual Withdrawal

*Peter Edwards**

Vietnam and Southeast Asia in 1968–69: A Lost Opportunity

. . . the [Australian] Government's Vietnam commitment was the product of two arguments. The first, commonly called the domino theory, rested on the assumptions that Asian communism was spreading, that it threatened Australian security, and that it would be expedient to meet the threat as early as possible and as far away as practicable [—Australia's forward defense policy]. The second theory, sometimes known as the insurance policy, assumed that the United States had nailed its colours to the mast in Vietnam and that Australia needed to support its great and powerful friend there to ensure that that friend would support it if it were ever threatened with attack. During 1968 and 1969 the international assumptions underlying the domino theory and the insurance policy were fundamentally challenged.

Many of the tensions in Southeast Asia during the early and mid-1960s had greatly eased. Anti-Communist governments, whether democratic, authoritarian or military, were now much stronger than they had been a few years earlier. The left-wing forces in Malaysia and Singapore were in disarray as the two countries were rapidly developing strong economic, political and social structures. Despite communal riots in Kuala Lumpur in 1969 both countries seemed destined for a secure and prosperous future. Thailand had also been thought vulnerable because of a communist insurgency in the northeast of the country near the border with Laos, but by the late 1960s coordinated civilian, military and police actions, aided by the burgeoning economy of Bangkok and the rest of the country, had deflated this threat. Similarly, communist insurgents in the Philippines no longer posed a serious threat. A principal aim of American policy in East and Southeast Asia was to ensure that Japan would be established as a stable and prosperous democracy with willing markets for its exports. By the late 1960s, the Japanese economy had recovered astonishingly successfully from the ruins of 1945 and was already being held up as an example for others to follow. Taiwan, South Korea and Hong Kong were similarly recording remarkable economic growth, all based on considerable reliance on market forces and strong private sectors rather than on the communist model of centrally directed industries. The most striking political change of all in the region was in Indonesia, where the anti-Communist forces under General Suharto were now firmly in control and determined to develop the economy in ways designed to win the confidence of Western governments and investors. The fate of both Laos and Cambodia was clearly linked to the outcome of the Vietnam War, but in global terms Indochina was now a largely isolated theatre of conflict, not the front line of a contest for all of Southeast Asia.

Moreover the great powers who stood to gain by promoting insurgencies were themselves in some difficulties. China's attention was turned inwards to its cultural revolution which, as Ky had told the Australian Cabinet in 1967, made it less likely to be involved in foreign adventures. The other major communist power, the Soviet Union, had severely damaged its international reputation by its military intervention in 1968 to crush the Czechoslovakian government which sought "socialism with a human face". By the end of the decade, the rift between China and the Soviet Union had passed from ideological rivalry to the brink of military conflict. The Soviets gave enormous publicity to a border incident at the Ussuri River in 1969, in which Chinese troops reportedly killed 23 Soviet frontier guards. The public and diplomatic ramifications of this clash demonstrated the degree to which both countries checked each other's power, opening the way for the United States and its allies to play them off against each other.

In many important ways, therefore, Australia's "period of gathering alarm", during which the Vietnam commitment had been made [in 1965] and publicly endorsed, was coming to an end. Moreover, there were many signs that policy-makers in Washington had noted the great changes in Southeast Asia between 1965 and 1969 and were drawing far-reaching conclusions about the directions of American policy. . . .

Of more immediate significance were the opinions of those who would direct American foreign policy from 1969 onwards. In late 1967 [in the journal *Foreign Affairs*] Richard Nixon, preparing his challenge for the Republican nomination, wrote of "Asia After Viet Nam" in terms broadly similar to those of [State Department Official William] Bundy. He noted the emerging political and economic strength of the non-communist Asian governments, arguing that the Vietnam commitment had done much to make this possible. It had, for example, "provided a shield behind which the anti-communist forces [in Indonesia] found the courage and the capacity to stage their counter-coup and, at the final moment, to rescue their country from the Chinese orbit". While thus defending the commitment, Nixon warned that "other nations must recognize that the role of the United States as world policeman is likely to be limited in the future". He described SEATO as anachronistic, foreshadowed an involvement with Asia that would be less military and more directed to social and economic development, and spoke of the need for "a satisfactory conclusion", rather than a crushing victory, in Vietnam. Some indication of what this might mean was given in an article [in *Foreign Affairs*] in January 1969, which discussed the terms on which a peace might be secured in Vietnam. It was written by Henry Kissinger, the Harvard professor who in the same month became President Richard Nixon's National Security Adviser, a position that he rapidly elevated in importance until it surpassed that of the Secretary of State. Kissinger, an authority on nineteenth-century European diplomatic history as well as current strategic issues, discussed the details of the peace negotiations without referring to the interest of allies such as Australia, but emphasizing that "However we got into Viet Nam . . . ending the war honorably is essential for the peace of the world".

These articles summarised a great deal of public and private discussion of American foreign policy. The consensus was that both the global balance between the great powers and the regional position in Southeast Asia were markedly different from what they had been just a few years earlier. Given the extent of domestic dissent over the war, the new

Republican administration would aim, with bipartisan support, to extricate itself from Vietnam, seeking an honorable solution rather than an unequivocal military victory. These changes fundamentally affected the two basic arguments that constituted the rationale for Australian involvement in the war. The domino theory had much less force, for the other "dominoes" now seemed much stronger and better able to withstand the impact of even an unfavorable outcome in Vietnam. The need to support the United States as an insurance policy was also weakened, since Indonesia no longer posed an imminent thereat to Australia, which might require American support under ANZUS [Australia-New Zealand-United States Security Treaty]; while the Americans were less able to demand the payment of a premium in Vietnam when they themselves were clearly intending to withdraw [gradually]. . . .

. . . As will be discussed in the next chapter, in June President Nixon announced the first withdrawal of American troops from Vietnam. A majority of the Australian people now appeared to believe that, if American troops could be withdrawn from this bitterly controversial war, then so could Australian troops.

From 1968 the Australian Government had to consider these major changes in global and regional politics, in the attitudes of American policy-makers, and in the mood of the Australian people. Together they constituted both a challenge and an opportunity. The old answers to the problems of Australian security, the familiar arguments of the domino theory and the insurance policy, were no longer adequate. The process of reassessment, started in late 1967 in reaction to the news of accelerated British withdrawal from east of Suez, should have led to new approaches. But the Australian Government remained unable until December 1972 to meet the new regional challenge or to take the opportunity to produce a foreign policy that would remove Vietnam as a focus for domestic division and dissent. Internationally, it seemed bewildered by uncertainty over American policy and especially by the British withdrawal, the effects of which were exaggerated in the minds of Australian ministers. . . . as the succeeding chapters will relate, the Australian Government continued for some years to rely on its traditional policies, even as their weaknesses became increasingly apparent. It missed an opportunity to exert some influence over the politics of the region and to defuse some of the discontent at home. Instead it allowed itself to be forced all too obviously to react to decisions taken elsewhere. . . .

During 1968 and 1969 Australian policy towards Vietnam was largely shaped by three events that took place in January 1968—the appointment of a new Australian Prime Minister, a major offensive by the communist forces in Vietnam, and a further acceleration in the withdrawal of British forces from east of Suez. First, the unexpected death of Harold Holt led, after a period of tension within and between the coalition parties while [John] McEwen served as Prime Minister, to the accession of John Grey Gorton to the prime ministership. . . .

The major objective of Australian foreign policy was to keep both Britain and the United States involved in Southeast Asia. Maintaining American involvement was the basis of Australia's commitment to Vietnam, but that involvement was called into question by the second key event of January 1968, the Tet offensive, launched by the People's Army of Viet Nam and the Viet Cong on 30 and 31 January, during the declared truce for the Tet (lunar New Year) holiday. The unexpected assault on most of the major cities and towns in South Vietnam was only the first part of a series of offensives designed to overcome the stalemate that the war had reached in 1967. The next nine months saw the fiercest fighting of the war, but the events of late January and early February had the greatest impact in the United States. . . . In his memoirs Johnson recalled warning the Australians that he "foresaw the North Vietnamese using 'kamikaze' tactics in the weeks ahead, committing their troops in a wave of suicide attacks". The Australian Cabinet papers recorded no such warning, but only mentioned the reference to the two North Vietnamese divisions, implying conventional rather than urban guerrilla warfare. Similarly, military assessments in January repeatedly foreshadowed the possibility of a major attack, but this was generally expected to be in the northern provinces of South Vietnam . . . . When the offensive came in the form of coordinated uprisings in cities and towns throughout South Vietnam, the authorities in Washington and Saigon could not conceal the fact that there had been a major intelligence failure.

. . . the fact that the communist forces had been able to mount such a widespread offensive after Johnson and Westmoreland had been making optimistic forecasts of military success cast further doubt on the credibility of official statements from Washington. Especially damning was the entry of nineteen Viet Cong guerrillas into the grounds of the American Embassy in Saigon. They were soon killed, but exaggerated reports that they had occupied the embassy buildings cast doubts on the

ability of the Americans and South Vietnamese to protect even their most sensitive locations. The sight, captured by still and television cameras and shown around the world, of the chief of the South Vietnamese police, General Nguyen Ngoc Loan, summarily executing a captured Viet Cong cadre—perhaps the most significant of the many memorable and influential images from the war—further undermined public confidence in the morality of the Western cause.

The immediate effect of the Tet offensive was two months of policy paralysis in Washington, culminating in an announcement by Lyndon Johnson on 31 March that he would stop the bombing of most of North Vietnam and withdraw from the 1968 presidential election. It was an admission that his policy had failed. Tet proved less of a turning point in American policy than was often stated at the time but it inflamed the widespread and growing doubts in the United States about the commitment. These doubts were profoundly important for Australian policy-makers. For the next several years, the making of Australian foreign policy would be based—as it had been in the period leading up to Johnson's unequivocal commitment to Vietnam in 1965—on uncertainty about the determination of the United States to remain militarily involved in Southeast Asia. . . .

. . . Tet and its impact dominated world news in early 1968, but the Australian Government had already received another shock—the third key event of January 1968— the implications of which were no less severe. In early January the British Government informed Australia, New Zealand, Malaysia and Singapore that British withdrawal from east of Suez would be even more rapid than had been foreshadowed in July 1967. All British forces would now leave Southeast Asia by 31 March 1971 and Britain no longer intended to maintain a special amphibious capability to intervene there if required. This development was profoundly disturbing to Canberra. Indeed, to judge by the amount of time spent in formal Cabinet discussions and the quantity of associated paperwork, the question of the impact of British withdrawal on Australian policy in Malaysia and Singapore was more important to Australian ministers than was the possible withdrawal of the United States from Vietnam. In fact the two were closely related, for the Australian Cabinet assumed that any future involvement in Malaysia and Singapore had to be acceptable to the United States, and that in turn depended on the future of American involvement in the region.

Australian policy-makers were mostly educated men of the generation who had fought for democracy in the world wars and who respected the military power and cultural values of the United Kingdom and the United States. They found the prospect that one, and possibly both, of Australia's great and powerful friends would withdraw from Southeast Asia profoundly disturbing. Uncertainty on this issue undermined their confidence in the basis of Australian defense policy. For the next five years Australian Government ministers wavered between reaffirming the traditional tenets of forward defense and seeking a new formula based on continental defense. . . .

The changing policies of Australia's great power allies challenged the new Prime Minister immediately he assumed office. When Gorton entered Parliament House after being sworn in at Government House on 10 January Lee Kuan Yew was waiting on the telephone. Singapore's Prime Minister had already met George Thomson, the United Kingdom Secretary of State for British Commonwealth Affairs, who was bringing the news of the latest British decision on withdrawal. . . .

. . . The Wilson Government's continuing economic problems had led to a devaluation of the pound sterling which made it imperative to reduce overseas defense expenditure further and therefore to accelerate the withdrawal from Asia. The Australian ministers, led by Gorton, [Paul] Hasluck and [Allen] Fairhall, expressed their "anxiety and dismay", trenchantly criticizing what Hasluck called 'a "little Europe" policy'. They set out their views in a five-page *aide-memoire* for Thomson to take to London, and press reports made their dissatisfaction plain. Although Thomson said he had been "deeply affected" by the force of the Australian views, Lee probably achieved more in his lone mission to London, where he persuaded the British to agree to delay the completion of the withdrawal to December instead of March 1971. This put it beyond the last possible date for the next British election, and Lee did not disguise his hope that a future Conservative government would adopt a different approach. In the event, the next election was in 1970, the Conservatives won, and Britain's east of Suez policy was in some respects modified. . . .

Almost immediately after returning from [a visit in late May to] Washington, Gorton went to Southeast Asia, visiting Vietnam, Singapore, Malaysia and Indonesia. Here . . . his public comments led reporters to characterize his views as hawkish. He told Australian troops at Nui Dat that his Government and 90 per cent of the Australian people were behind them, even though "the newspapers tend to give publicity to any nut who carries a placard or sits in the middle of a road"; and he spoke deprecatingly of the "things that are called peace talks in

Paris", emphasizing that they were only preliminary discussions, to assess whether there was a basis for serious negotiations.

While critics of the Vietnam commitment protested at being dismissed as "nuts", Gorton's forthright and outspoken style remained popular with many Australians. . . .

The Guam Doctrine and Pressure for Withdrawal of Troops

. . . Richard Nixon, who was elected President in November 1968 and took office in January 1969, was committed to seeking "peace with honour" in Vietnam. The growing unpopularity of the war in the United States encouraged him to "bring the boys home" but at the same time he had to avoid the accusation of deserting America's allies. As he had foreshadowed in his 1967 article in *Foreign Affairs*, he argued that America's allies would have to do more in their own defense if they were to receive support from the United States. After he commented along these lines to reporters in Guam in July 1969 during a visit to several Asian countries, Nixon's view became known as the Guam doctrine. It created considerable nervousness in the capitals of allied countries, not least in Saigon and Canberra, because Nixon was known to be especially reluctant to become engaged again in a land war in Asia.

Gorton visited Washington twice in early 1969 when the general direction of Nixon's policies was already apparent. . . . Reports from Washington indicated that he had developed as high an admiration for Nixon as Holt had towards Johnson, and the public expression of this regard was regrettably similar. At a dinner at the White House, apparently seeking to reassure his host of the strength of the alliance while sounding genuinely Australian for the benefit of his domestic audience, he said that "wherever the United States is resisting aggression . . . then we will go Waltzing Matilda with you". News of Gorton's slogan was generally received not so much with the outrage that had attended Holt's "all the way with LBJ" as with derision. Commentators noted that if the statement were to be taken at face value it committed Australia to support the United States not just in the Asia-Pacific region but anywhere in the world. One newspaper editorial wondered: "Whatever happens to Australian Prime Ministers in Washington?"

On his return Gorton assured Parliament that Nixon had given him strong assurances of the continuing support of the United States for its commitments under ANZUS and SEATO. . . .

After a meeting with the RVN's [Republic of Vietnam's] President

[Nguyen Van] Thieu at Midway, Nixon announced in June that an initial contingent of 25,000 American troops would be withdrawn from Vietnam. The Australian commitment, and the Australian Government's drifting defense policy, were immediately brought under renewed pressure. Gorton was advised of Nixon's decision only a matter of hours before its announcement but it was sufficient to prepare him for the inevitable calls to begin a comparable Australian withdrawal. The Prime Minister said that an Australian troop reduction would be unfair to the United States as the American withdrawal was made possible by the increased capacity of the South Vietnamese forces and not by an agreement with the communists to reduce forces on both sides. Speaking on television, Gorton also noted that the Australian task force was self-contained, and to withdraw parts of it would be "militarily quite ridiculous". Nevertheless Gorton gave the impression that neither the United States Government nor his political allies in Australia would allow him to change policy direction. In late September the Nixon administration announced the withdrawal of another 35,000 American troops, but the governments of the other five troop-contributing counties—Australia, New Zealand, Thailand, the Republic of Korea and the Philippines—said they had no plans to remove any forces. American officials let it be known that for both political and military reasons they wanted their allies to remain at full strength.

After Nixon's first announcement, officials in Defence, External Affairs and the service departments discussed the possibility of Australian troop withdrawals. Army representatives in particular argued strongly that the task force, comprising three battalions with supporting forces, was a balanced unit, and that to reduce it by one battalion would be dangerous. They pressed the case that if one battalion were withdrawn, all should be withdrawn. . . . Partial withdrawal of the Australian task force was thus ruled out—and the Government was not yet prepared to consider "all out". The war was far from over: tens of thousands of American troops and even larger numbers of Vietnamese soldiers and civilians on both sides would be killed before all American forces were withdrawn. Nevertheless, the direction of Nixon's policy was clear. Under what his Defense Secretary, Melvin Laird, called "Vietnamisation", the emphasis would be on removing American forces in the ostensible belief that the forces of the Republic of Vietnam were increasingly capable of bearing the burden. Gorton had evidently achieved a good rapport with the new President but he was unable to offer the Australian people any relief from the continuing demands of the increasingly unpopular war. The "Waltzing Matilda" statement made him politically vulnerable to the accusation that he was too willing to accept the commitments recommended by Washington, even when the United States itself was beginning to reduce its own overseas involvements. . . .

On the evening of 15 December (American time) [1969] Nixon announced a further reduction of the American troop ceiling by 50,000. At the same time, the morning of 16 December in Australia, Gorton issued a press statement which said that "when the military situation in Vietnam permits the next substantial withdrawal, then, in consultation with the Government of the Republic of Vietnam, some Australian units will be included in the numbers scheduled for such withdrawal". Gorton noted that he had talked with Nixon, who had said he was happy to agree with this view. Gorton did not hold a press conference or brief journalists to clarify details of the decision, but in the evening made a statement on radio and television designed to dampen some of the speculation on troop withdrawals. Looking ill-tempered and uncomfortable, the Prime Minister emphasized that all that had been reached was an agreement in principle. He stressed that . . . there was no decision on how large any Australian withdrawals might be. It was the beginning of the end of the Vietnam commitment, but all too obviously it was an immediate reaction to an American announcement, not the first phase of a carefully considered Australian defense strategy. . . .

. . . on 20 April [1970] Nixon announced the withdrawal of a further 150,000 American troops over the following year, bringing the total reduction in the United States troop levels since Nixon had taken office to 265,500. The Australians, like many officials in Washington, had expected the President to announce another reduction in the tens of thousands over a few months but had not anticipated such a dramatic gesture. It prompted a quick response from the Australian Government. After reassessing Cabinet's decision of the previous month, Gorton announced on 22 April in a press statement and a speech to Parliament that Australia would make its first troop withdrawal by not replacing 8 RAR [one battalion] in November. . . .

My Lai, Cambodia, and Kent State, 1969–70

. . . For much of 1969 the impact of the American anti-war movement had been blunted by the initial withdrawals ordered by President Nixon, but towards the end of the year it collected its forces for a new series of major demonstrations. Its leaders called on the American people to observe a 'Moratorium' on 15 October. Hitherto a moratorium meant an authorised delay in the payment of a debt. The anti-war movement took up the word to indicate a refusal to accept 'business as usual' as long as the war continued, while avoiding the negative connotations of 'strike'. The response in 1200 cities and towns far exceeded the organisers' expectations, with estimates of the numbers involved ranging from 500,000 to several millions. A month later the organisers joined forces with a more radical group, the New Mobilization Committee to End the War in Vietnam, to organise a 'march against death' in Washington. Supported by more than 250 000 people, it was the largest demonstration ever seen in the national capital. 'It looked like the Russian revolution', observed Nixon's Attorney-General.

Just before the 'march against death,' the first newspaper reports appeared of what was to become known as the My Lai massacre. In March 1968 a company of about 120 American soldiers had killed several hundred civilians, including old men, women and children, in a hamlet known to the Americans as My Lai 4, part of Song My (or Son My) village in Quang Ngai province. The savage killings, accompanied by rapes and other brutalities, had been under investigation by American military authorities for nearly eighteen months but had not previously been reported. Within a week the impact of the story was augmented by stomach-turning photographs. Around the world, protesters took the accounts of My Lai as confirmation of their view that the Vietnam War was not a crusade but an atrocity. The reaction in Britain, particularly from the left wing of the Labour Party, was even stronger than that in the United States.

My Lai confirmed the view of Australian dissenters that their country had placed itself on the wrong side of an immoral war. Images of My Lai became common on anti-war publicity. . . .

International events . . . raised the emotional temperature. In March [1970] the Cambodian head of state, Prince Norodom Sihanouk, who had maintained a delicate and increasingly difficult balancing act between the Americans and the Vietnamese communists, was deposed by his own Government, led by Prime Minister General Lon Nol, and the National Assembly. The Cambodians wanted the North Vietnamese and Viet Cong to stop using territory in the east of Cambodia as sanctuaries; since early 1969, the Americans had conducted a clandestine bombing program against these sanctuaries, but had not intervened with ground forces. After Sihanouk's fall the North Vietnamese and Viet Cong rapidly expanded their control of Cambodian territory westwards, threatening the security of the capital, Phnom Penh. On 30 April (1 May in Australian time) Nixon announced that the Americans and South Vietnamese had launched a joint incursion into Cambodia aimed at clearing out the sanctuaries and destroying the elusive headquarters of the communists' operations in South Vietnam.

The American intervention in Cambodia could not have been worse timed for the Australian Government, which had not been consulted about it. Only days earlier [Australian Foreign Minister William] McMahon had announced Australia's support for a call by the Indonesian Foreign Minister, Adam Malik, for a conference of foreign ministers of several Asian and Pacific countries, to support the preservation of Cambodia's independence and neutrality, non-intervention in the country by external powers, and the reactivation of the International Control Commission established under the 1954 Geneva Agreements. After discussions with Gorton and McEwen, McMahon had issued a long and detailed statement on 27 April, discussing developments in Cambodia and supporting the Indonesian approach. Cabinet endorsed his position on 30 April, the day before the American-South Vietnamese military operation was announced. The following day, after the shock of Nixon's announcement, Cabinet decided to proceed with participation in the conference, but also expressed sympathy with the American decision. There was a noticeable pause before Australia officially declared its position, but on 5 May Gorton made a statement in Parliament which noted that Australian forces were not, and were not likely to become, involved in Cambodia, but which defended the American-South Vietnamese action and rebutted Opposition criticisms. . . . Australia was once more publicly identified as a close ally and supporter of controversial American military action in Indochina, overshadowing its involvement in a diplomatic initiative through which Asian and Pacific countries were seeking a regional solution to the Cambodian problem. . . .

. . . In the United States the anti-war movement had once more been declining. Now, it seemed, Nixon had suddenly widened the war to include a previously neutral country. Moreover, the Cambodian incursion followed soon after revelations that American military involvement in Laos, especially bombing, had been far more extensive than the public or the Congress had previously been told. Universities erupted in widespread protests, many of which involved arson, violence and destruction. During a demonstration on 4 May at Kent State University in Ohio, National Guardsmen opened fire without orders and without warning. Four students were killed. In the United States the first deaths directly associated with Vietnam protests evoked an emotional response perhaps even greater than that elicited by the My Lai massacre. . . .

Withdrawal from Vietnam, 1971–72

The Vietnam War now receded gradually from the centre-stage of Australian politics. The Government was clearly set on the course of withdrawal, but choosing the appropriate rate posed considerable difficulties. As Robert O'Neill, an astute observer who had served as an intelligence officer in Vietnam, noted:

> Too fast a rate of withdrawal could have caused an embarrassingly rapid collapse of South Vietnamese government authority in Phuoc Tuy Province. Too slow a rate could have offered a target for a new round of moratorium demonstrations, making the government look increasingly out of touch with reality, and, if withdrawal were deferred too long, possible deterioration of the situation in South Vietnam might have complicated matters.

The problem of how to pace withdrawal from Vietnam was increasingly overshadowed by other developments in international politics, especially major changes in the attitude of the United States and its allies towards the communist People's Republic of China. In July 1971 President Nixon announced, to worldwide astonishment, that he had accepted an invitation to visit the People's Republic, starting an inexorable movement by Western countries towards diplomatic recognition of the state that several governments, including Australia's, had long regarded as the principal source of many of the world's ills, not least the Vietnam War. In October the People's Republic became a member of the United Nations, taking the permanent seat in the Security Council previously held by the anti-communist Republic of China which still controlled only the island of Taiwan. . . .

. . . On 30 March [1971, the new Prime Minister] McMahon, in one of his first major statements as Prime Minister, announced this second withdrawal of Australian troops from Vietnam, bringing the level of

Australian forces to about 6000 men, compared with its peak of about 8000 in 1968–70. As Cabinet had agreed, McMahon noted that the withdrawals would take place gradually over four to six months, beginning in May. When, as expected, Nixon announced on 8 April a further withdrawal of American troops, McMahon simply referred to his own announcement of a few days earlier, deflecting pressure for a more rapid withdrawal.

. . . The Government had thus laid down a strategy for a slow withdrawal of the Australian forces in Vietnam, under which the two-battalion task force would remain at least until the end of 1971. The Australian announcement had preceded Washington's, breaking the pattern of Australian responses to American decisions, and the reductions were sufficient to ease domestic criticism. Nevertheless, they had not been enough for some. Several editorials, in newspapers that had long supported the commitment, urged the Government to abandon its "dilatory, piecemeal approach" and to end Australia's "military misadventure in Vietnam" by bringing all the troops home as soon as possible. Events over the following months would reinforce those calls. . . .

This proposal for an orderly and graduated withdrawal was overtaken by unforeseen events. Whitlam, in a bold step for a Leader of the Opposition, visited communist China in July 1971 before Nixon was to do so, and was publicly received by the Premier, Zhou Enlai. On 12 July McMahon told a meeting of Young Liberals: "I find it incredible that at a time when Australian soldiers are still engaged in Vietnam, the leader of the Labor Party is becoming a spokesman for those against whom we are fighting". Although he had mentioned this speech beforehand to the American Embassy he was given no hint that, at the same time as Whitlam, Nixon's National Security Adviser Henry Kissinger had also been in Beijing preparing for the President's announcement, to be made on 15 July . . . What the Japanese called the Nixon *shokku* [shock] also had a cataclysmic impact on Australian politics . . . On 26 July Cabinet reviewed the withdrawal of forces from Vietnam "in the light of the development in United States policy" implied by Nixon's proposed visit to Beijing. Cabinet decided that "there could be no assumption that the United States would not now speed up its own program of withdrawal", and consequently "that it should move immediately to withdraw and to do so to an 'accelerated' timetable". The two battalions of the task force would be withdrawn in October and December 1971. Two days later, before any consultations had been held with the South Vietnamese, American or New Zealand authorities, McMahon told the state council of the Liberal Party that Australian troops were likely to be withdrawn within six months.

After discussions with the allies McMahon announced to Parliament on the second day of the next session, 18 August, that the Government had decided to withdraw all remaining combat forces from Vietnam. He made no reference to Nixon's policy towards China, but placed the decision in the context of the improved security situation in Vietnam, especially Phuoc Tuy province, and the improved capacity of the South Vietnamese forces. He did not give a detailed timetable, but said: "Most of the combat elements will be home in Australia by Christmas 1971". Australian policy had clearly changed markedly since Gorton had assured President Thieu in March that no battalions would be withdrawn before the end of that year. Nevertheless, on this occasion no minister visited Saigon for consultations and Thieu was informed of the decision only two days before the announcement. South Vietnamese authorities were known to be dismayed at the short notice and minimal consultation, but they now had little sympathy in the Australian press or public opinion.

The news summarized in the headline "Troops Home By Christmas" was welcomed with a sense of relief which overshadowed all other considerations. . . .

The decision taken by Cabinet on 26 July and announced by McMahon on 18 August marked the imminent end of Australia's military involvement in the Vietnam War. Leaders of the anti-war movement such as John Lloyd . . . claimed it as a great victory for "domestic political pressures within Australia", especially the "huge Moratorium rallies". Whitlam, by contrast, asserted that: "There is one reason and one reason only why Australia is now withdrawing. We are getting out because the US is getting out". The Government was reluctant to admit that domestic pressures played any part in its decision-making, although Tom Hughes, now out of the Ministry, referred to "a distinct change in the climate of public opinion" which had "heavily undermined" public support for the Government's policies. Hughes also noted "the insensitivity—to use a mild word—of those whom we have sought to help to the necessity of respecting the values that intervention had been designed to protect". Current political manoeuvres, which would ensure that President Thieu had no effective opposition in the election on 3 October, together with the widespread reports of corruption in Saigon, had greatly reduced the Government's ability or inclination to present the Republic of Vietnam as a threatened bastion of democracy. Nor was the Government's reference to the improved situation in Phuoc Tuy province without foundation, as security there had improved greatly, although statements about the strength of the South Vietnamese forces were made with more hope than confidence. Robert O'Neill concluded that the Government's adoption of a rapid rate of withdrawal was based predominately on a desire "to cut its political losses on Vietnam" before the 1972 election. Certainly McMahon, who had always been more sensitive to domestic political pressures than to strategic concerns, had moved as quickly as possible to implement the "new thought" on Australian involvement that he had described as necessary soon after his elevation to the Prime Ministership.

Despite the enormous attention given at this time to policy towards China, few political observers linked Australia's Vietnam decision directly to Nixon's dramatic announcement on China. Yet, according to the Cabinet record, this was the critical factor in the decision to adopt an "accelerated" withdrawal. It is possible that the "Nixon shock" was used by ministers who wanted a rapid withdrawal, including McMahon, to overcome the reluctance of some of their colleagues. Nevertheless the wording of the Cabinet record, so soon after McMahon's speech of 12 July which identified the Chinese with "those against whom we are fighting", suggests that he may have taken seriously the rhetorical assertion that the Vietnamese communists were acting at China's instigation, an assumption that had long been abandoned by the Americans. If so, there was at least a symmetry in Australia's commitment. Just as Menzies had included in his 1965 announcement an ill-judged reference to "a thrust by Communist China between the Indian and Pacific Oceans", so McMahon was basing the 1971 withdrawal on the enormous change in American, and consequently the West's, policies towards China. . . .

. . . At a press conference just before leaving Australia [to visit Washington] he [McMahon] was asked about reports that the Americans had "secretly sounded out" the Australian Government over a proposal to send Australian military advisers into Cambodia to train the Cambodian army. McMahon replied that he knew of no such suggestions, adding gratuitously "I would have known as soon as anyone". Over the succeeding days two facts emerged. First, the American Embassy in Canberra had approached the Australian Government in April along these lines; the then Ministers for Foreign Affairs (Bury) and Defense (Gorton) had rejected the proposal in accordance with a policy of not becoming militarily involved in Cambodia, and McMahon had been informed. Second, on 30 September an officer of the Embassy had raised with a

Foreign Affairs official the possibility that Australia, with New Zealand, might join the Americans in training Cambodian forces at training camps in Phuoc Tuy province in Vietnam; no word of this reached McMahon until his Defense Minister, Fairbairn, sent him a letter just before his departure, which McMahon did not see until after his arrival in the United States. Cabinet then proceeded to decide in favour of the proposal on 2 November and the Prime Minister was in the humiliating position of having to consult his Cabinet in Australia to discover their decision in case the matter was raised in his principal business meeting with Nixon. . . .

. . . In 1972, ugly violence reasserted its predominance. With all Australian combat forces withdrawn, the anti-war and anti-conscription groups were becoming confined to a hard core of committed activists, who demonstrated three weaknesses which reinforced one another. They became increasingly divided over tactics and ideology, with the moderates no longer able to maintain control over the extreme elements; they were more likely to use violence against people and property; and they were losing community support.

At the same time the war itself took on a markedly different character. On 30 March [1972] the North Vietnamese Army, the PAVN [People's Army of Vietnam], began a major offensive. Several divisions, supported by artillery and tanks, crossed the Demilitarised Zone and the Cambodian border and advanced quickly towards major cities in South Vietnam. For years, when the Government had said that the war was an attack by the North on the South, critics had responded that it was a guerrilla war by the Viet Cong—the communist-led rebels in the South—against the government in Saigon. There was evidence enough for both views but the 1968 Tet offensive had cost the Viet Cong much more severe losses than it had the PAVN . . .

That South Vietnam might fall to this offensive was unacceptable to the United States Government, although the withdrawal of American forces continued even as the offensive was being prepared. In April Nixon increased air attacks on targets in the North. On 8 May he announced a step that had long been mooted but considered too dangerous: the entrances to North Vietnamese ports would be mined to prevent the entry of supplies, especially those from the Soviet Union. Critics of the administration denounced the step but, after days of immense tension, the Soviet leaders proceeded with a long-planned summit meeting with Nixon in Moscow. The diplomacy of the President and Kissinger towards the communist powers had proved more sophisticated and effective than that of previous administrations, with which Australian Governments had been uncritically aligned. . . .

. . . In this context, with the Australian troops and all but about 60,000 of the United States forces withdrawn, the demonstrations were widely interpreted as explicit support for a communist victory, despite assertions by organisers that they were directed against all forms of war . . . .

Amid the battles [in demonstrations] on Australian city streets one casualty went largely unnoticed—calm analysis of the nature of the war in Vietnam. The North Vietnamese offensive had quite changed the character of the war. Peasant guerrillas, regarded as heroes by many protesters, had little part in events. The offensive was a classic, conventional invasion which the South Vietnamese forces, with considerable aid from American air and naval power, succeeded in resisting. While Australians condemned the violence in their cities, few stopped to consider the implications for the war itself. By this time, Australia had withdrawn all but advisory forces and . . . there was no likelihood that any combat forces would be returned.

. . . The declining authority of the McMahon Government had been matched by the descent and disintegration of the protest movement. . . . the protests in April and May 1972 degenerated into violent confrontations . . . they had lost the support of the general community, which was more concerned with the prospect of the first federal Labor [Party] government in 23 years.

. . . Although the Vietnam War and conscription had not been much discussed during the 1972 election campaign, they were extremely important to those who had been involved in the protests. In one election-day survey, only 1 in 25 of those who had voted Labor nominated these subjects as the reason for their vote, but this low percentage still placed the war and conscription ahead of any other single issue. . . .

. . . Whitlam was especially determined to keep close control over foreign policy, and few decisions in this field ever came to Cabinet. For his first eleven months as Prime Minister, Whitlam was also Minister for Foreign Affairs. Even after he formally handed this portfolio to a trusted colleague, Senator D.R. Willesee (WA) [Western Australia], Whitlam ensured that his own hand shaped all major aspects of Australian foreign policy. His instincts were reformist rather than radical. He was determined to change Australian foreign policy from resistance of communist expansion to what he later described as "the intelligent anticipation of change", and defense policy from forward defense to the "logic and independence" of continental defense. Old alliances with the

United Kingdom and the United States were to remain but Australia would assert that it was an ally rather than a province of London or Washington, while coldness towards Moscow, Beijing and Hanoi would thaw. But he did not want to damage Australia's relations with Washington, nor to close American defense installations in Australia, for he accepted the value of Australia's defense relationship with the United States.

The "Christmas Bombing" of Hanoi, December 1972

Developments in the Vietnam War would make this balance between alliance and independence exceptionally difficult to achieve. In the last months of 1972 Nixon, who was re-elected President in a landslide in November, and Henry Kissinger, who would become Secretary of State in the second Nixon administration, were seeking to negotiate a peace agreement with the DRV government, to achieve Nixon's goal of "peace with honour". In October Hanoi adopted a more positive attitude in negotiations, accepting that the Thieu regime in Saigon could remain after a cease-fire. On 26 October, twelve days before the United States presidential election, Kissinger announced that "we believe peace is at hand", but in December both Hanoi and Saigon raised new difficulties. To put pressure on Hanoi and to reassure Saigon, Nixon ordered that Haiphong harbour be mined and that military targets in the Hanoi-Haiphong area be bombed. During eleven days, from 18 to 29 December with the exception of Christmas Day, American aircraft dropped more bombs in this area than they had in all Indochina during the previous three years. In early January the DRV negotiators withdrew many of their demands and accepted American suggestions that they had previously rejected. On 23 January 1973 the American and DRV negotiators initialled a peace agreement, which was signed by four parties—the United States, the DRV, and RVN, and the Provisional Revolutionary Government established in South Vietnam by the NLF—on 27 January, the day a cease-fire came into effect.

Before the bombing evidently achieved its goal of bringing an end to the fighting, it had provoked an enormous outburst of condemnation around the world. It was in fact more accurately confined to military and industrial targets than critics assumed and cost far fewer civilian lives than the bombing of German and Japanese cities in the 1939–45 war, to which it was often compared. Nevertheless, encouraged by reports that wrongly suggested that civilian areas of Hanoi had been "carpet-bombed" with mindless barbarity, peoples and governments around the world called it the "Christmas bombing" and charged Nixon with having resumed the war by the indiscriminate mass murder of civilians. "The moral indignation", remembered Kissinger, "rose with each day". The Swedish Government compared the Nixon administration to Hitler's, and opinion in Congress turned even more strongly against the war and the Nixon administration.

The bombing presented Whitlam with an opportunity to demonstrate his new approach to the relationship with the United States. Publicly he was restrained, telling a press conference on 19 December only that he would like to see the negotiations resumed. But on the following day Whitlam sent a personal letter to Nixon through the Australian Embassy in Washington. He said that the breakdown in negotiations with North Vietnam was "a bitter blow" to the Australian Government and people, and questioned "most earnestly" whether the bombing would bring the North Vietnamese to the negotiating table. Praising Kissinger and the American negotiators for their patience and resolve, Whitlam said that he was moved "as much by a positive and . . . helpful desire to put negotiations back on the rails" as by distress at a particular aspect of American foreign policy, and for this reason intended to approach heads of some governments in the Asia-Pacific region to address a joint appeal to the United States and North Vietnam to resume serious negotiations. Whitlam said that he would not release the text of the letter, although its existence might become publicly known, and he assured Nixon that he looked forward "to a period of positive cooperation . . . on a wide range of matters" between Canberra and Washington.

Nixon was infuriated by this first communication from the leader of a country that had until now been America's staunchest ally in Indochina and whose Prime Ministers had hitherto waltzed all the way with their great and powerful friend in the White House. He disdained to answer the letter, and grouped Australia with Sweden as his least-favoured Western governments. The tensions were inflamed by a series of increasingly vitriolic statements by some left-wing ministers in the new Government. Tom Uren, the Minster for Urban and Regional Development, condemned Nixon's and Kissinger's "mentality of thuggery". Dr. [J. F.] Cairns, the Minister for Trade and Industry and the third-ranking member of the Government, first said that the bombing indicated that Nixon had no intention to end the war. A few days later he publicly condemned the bombing of Hanoi as "the most brutal, indiscriminating slaughter of defenceless men, women and children in living memory", said that American policy was the deceitful and morally bankrupt product of corrupt men who had never been elected, and called on the public to protest. Clyde Cameron, the Minster for Labour, called the Christmas bombing the most monstrous act in the history of the human race, and speculated that it must be the policy of maniacs. Outside the Ministry a Labor Senator, Arthur Gietzelt, proposed that the Government seize land owned by American companies in Australia, close American bases, refuse entry to any American not in a peace movement, and move to have the United States expelled from the United Nations.

These statements were widely criticised. There were small but violent demonstrations in Sydney against the bombing and the windows of the Pan American Airways office were smashed once more but, with Australians no longer serving in Vietnam, there was little public support for protests . . . Leading members of the Waterside Workers' Federation and the Seamen's Union warned that, if the bombing continued, they would refuse to service American ships trying to dock in Australian ports and ban the entry of American goods, but not passengers, to Australia. As maritime unions around Australia began resolving to join the ban, American waterside unions, which had close links with the Nixon administration, retaliated by banning the entry of Australian ships into American ports. Two-thirds of Australia's export trade to the United States was threatened.

As the rhetorical outbursts threatened to turn into serious industrial strife, there were tense exchanges between Australian and American officials in both Washington and Canberra. The Americans evidently found it difficult to accept the Australians' explanations that the left-wing ministers were expressing personal, not official, views and that the unions were not acting at the Government's behest. They were further disturbed when [Lance] Barnard announced on 27 December that the Australian Government would cancel all military aid to South Vietnam, little of which had been spent anyway, and abandon the McMahon Government's plan to train Cambodian troops in Australia, although civil aid to Saigon would continue.

Whitlam faced an acute dilemma in shaping his reaction to the bombing. His attempt to coordinate a joint statement by Australia, Indonesia and Japan had come to nothing. On 28 December he held a wide-ranging discussion with Sir James Plimsoll, the [Australian] Ambassador to the United States who had returned to Canberra for consultations, and other senior advisers. Whitlam said that he did not wish to express views on matters that were beyond Australia's capacity to control, but he believed that the bombing was intolerable and militarily futile. He thought that American policies on Vietnam for the past ten years had been misconceived and said that he was essentially neutral towards Hanoi and Saigon. The new Prime Minister said that he did not wish to appear to be gloating over the failures or mistakes of his predecessors, . . . but he wanted the public to know his views on the bombing. Plimsoll said that Nixon and Kissinger had sought to get the United States out of the war without sowing the seeds of an American form of fascism, like that which had developed in Germany after 1918. He also noted that military intervention in Vietnam had seemed right to a generation that had grown up on the supposed lessons of the 1930s. Whitlam said the parallels between pre-1939 fascism and post-1945 communism had always been false. He was strongly opposed to prolongation of the war or continuation of the bombing, but apart from the "intractable question" of Vietnam, he saw no other points of difficulty with the United States. Indeed he wanted the Americans to know that he was anxious to see the United States constructively involved in Asia, especially with development assistance . . .

Whitlam's anger and frustration at the course of events emerged in a meeting with the American Ambassador in Canberra, Walter Rice, on 8 January. As the dispassionate official record stated, Whitlam "spoke virtually without interruption for 45 minutes". In vigorous terms he told Rice that any Australian reactions to the bombing were far less important than the bombing itself. His Government had been voted in with a mandate to do all it could to end the war and Australian participation in it. His letter to Nixon had been in accord with that mandate. Australia wanted to maintain good relations with the United States. His own view was that the American defence installations in Australia did not harm Australia and could help the United States, but if Washington attempted "to screw us or bounce us", the retention of these facilities "would become a matter of contention". The fact that negotiations with Hanoi had recommenced meant that he would continue to be "very discreet and restrained" in his public comments; otherwise he would have used words like "atrocious" and "barbarous" to the press.

The tension subsided quickly after the bombing stopped. Whitlam reprimanded Cairns, Cameron and Uren, ensuring, as he later wrote, "that the maverick Ministers did not speak again outside their ministerial responsibilities". In collaboration with the ACTU [Australian Council of Trade Unions] president, Hawke, he had the maritime unions call off their ban on American shipping, without loss of face to the unionists. Whitlam let it be known that he had written to Nixon, but as promised he did not reveal his letter's text.

The Christmas bombing had severely strained Australian-American relations, but it had also allowed Whitlam to declare that he was opposed to any continuation of the war while hoping to maintain close relations with the United States on other issues. The substance and conduct of his diplomacy, contrasting with the statements of his left-wing colleagues, reaffirmed his personal control over foreign policy. But the episode also indicated that the Australian people were rapidly losing interest in Vietnam. In late January, some of the last demonstrations against the war were held. Few attended; the press ignored them. Some militants had hoped that mass protest would be maintained and directed towards other political and social questions but, with conscription ended and all Australian troops out of Vietnam, the Moratorium movement was effectively over. . . .

The "Peace Agreement," 1973–74

The conclusion of the peace agreement on 27 January [1973] opened the way for the establishment of relations. Plimsoll, now returned to Washington, warned Whitlam that a formal announcement of relations with Hanoi would be "bound to touch a raw nerve in the White House" and recommended proceeding slowly. At the same time, he also noted that to establish relations with Hanoi while maintaining an embassy in Saigon could be seen as endorsing Saigon's view that Vietnam comprised two states within one temporarily divided nation, rather than Hanoi's claim to be the sole legitimate government. In public discussion of the topic in subsequent days, much was made of this point, as well as the Government's intention to give generous aid to all of Vietnam.

On 2 February Australia's Ambassador to France, Alan Renouf, was instructed to approach the DRV's representatives in Paris with a view to establishing relations with Hanoi, but not at the price of severing relations with Saigon or ceasing aid to South Vietnam. In deference to concern in Washington, the approach was delayed until Kissinger had visited Hanoi and received an assurance on the DRV's commitment to the peace agreement. On 13 February Renouf made the first official contact. Initially it appeared that the DRV would readily accept the Australian proposal to announce the establishment of diplomatic relations without mentioning recognition, but on 19 February the DRV negotiator stated that Hanoi insisted that the announcement should refer to "reciprocal recognition". Renouf demurred, then agreed, on the understanding that the Australian Government would, if challenged, state that it recognised the DRV with respect to North Vietnam and the RVN with respect to South Vietnam. Canberra confirmed Renouf's decision. On 26 February Whitlam announced that Australia and the DRV had decided upon reciprocal recognition and the establishment of diplomatic relations, noting that this did not alter Australia's relations with the RVN or its representation in Saigon. Opinion polls indicated that most Australians either favoured or were undecided about the new relationship. During the negotiations, Renouf asked for information about five Australians—two airmen, two soldiers and a journalist—missing in Indochina, but the DRV offered no assistance. There were few diplomatic repercussions from the announcement. The Australian Embassy in Hanoi was opened under a charge d'affaires in July 1973, with the first ambassador taking up his post in March 1975. . . .

Despite Whitlam's declaration of the importance of ties with America, the decisions and especially the rhetoric that emerged from his Government, particularly concerning Vietnam, soured relations between Canberra and Washington. In July 1973 Whitlam visited the United States and was received, probably coolly, by Nixon and Kissinger. Criticism of the American defence facilities in Australia by Labor's left wing exacerbated the tension and for a time American intelligence treated the Whitlam Government as potentially hostile. The Nixon administration's concern grew after the Government was re-elected on 18 May 1974 and Cairns became Deputy Prime Minister. As part of a wider review of the American relationship with Australia, Nixon ordered the Central Intelligence Agency to consider whether the defense facilities should be relocated to another country. But such concern was already fading as Nixon became preoccupied with defending himself against accusations that he had electronically eavesdropped on colleagues and opponents, a practice born from his anger that news of the secret bombing of Cambodia had become public. His resignation in August 1974 cleared the air, and Whitlam's visit to the United States in October 1974 took place in a more cordial atmosphere than his first. Australian commentators believed that Washington had developed a new respect for a loyal, but independently minded, ally.

. . . The peace agreement permitted units of Hanoi's army, the PAVN, to remain in areas of South Vietnam that they dominated, allowing the Provisional Revolutionary Government to claim control of large areas. Nixon had promised that American power would save its ally if Hanoi broke the peace agreement and invaded the South, but Congress was tiring of supporting the anti-communist cause in Indochina. American military aid to Saigon dwindled, and Nixon's resignation ended any possibility that the United States would spend further blood and treasure in Vietnam. In January 1975, the PAVN began what it called the "Ho Chi Minh offensive", which cut rapidly through the northern and central provinces of South Vietnam, reaching the outskirts of Saigon by April.

Saigon's Fall, 1975

Nowhere in the South were there popular uprisings in support of the communists. Instead, thousands fled from the battle zones, creating floods of refugees within South Vietnam. Nevertheless, Whitlam and several of his ministers believed that Hanoi's imminent victory was firm evidence that the communist cause had always been the more popular and therefore the more legitimate. They were determined that Australia should keep its good relations with Hanoi and wipe away the embarrassment of having for so long supported the wrong side. At the same time they recognised that many Australians did not share their sympathies, and they felt obliged to insist that the 1973 peace agreement be observed. On 12 March Whitlam sent letters to the two Vietnamese governments, urging them to negotiate with each other. He told Hanoi that it could not blame Saigon entirely for the war's renewal, and told Saigon that it could not entirely blame Hanoi. The letters were balanced and almost identical in substance. . . .

By . . . [April] officials in Foreign Affairs were arguing that to call on both sides to adhere to the peace agreement would only serve Saigon's goal of keeping Vietnam divided, which was "not Hanoi's purpose and should not be Australia's", and "that military pressure" was "the only way" to change the situation. On 2 April Whitlam approved drafts by Foreign Affairs for cabled instructions to Australia's Ambassadors in Saigon and Hanoi. The difference between the two cables, sent that day, was pronounced. [Geoffrey] Price in Saigon was instructed to press Thieu to negotiate and to begin the process to reunify Vietnam, as only reunification would bring a real end to the war. [David] Wilson in

Hanoi was to say that Australia "would like to see in Saigon a government which will genuinely negotiate for reunification"; that it understood Hanoi's frustration with Thieu's intransigence; that Hanoi should "make it clear" that the renewal of fighting was merely an attempt to enforce the peace agreement, not an attempt to break it; and that fighting would cease once Thieu accepted his obligations. Unlike Price, Wilson was also to offer generous post-war aid. Unlike the letters of 12 March, the cables of 2 April were clearly more sympathetic to Hanoi than to Saigon. Astute observers noted that neither the DRV nor the RVN would pay much heed to the Australian communications. . . .

. . . Whitlam could no longer resist the public pressure. As well as deciding to close the Embassy, he agreed to grant entry to three categories of adult Vietnamese: husbands, wives and children of non-official Australians; husbands, wives and children of Vietnamese students currently in Australia; and Vietnamese who had been closely associated with the Australian presence in Vietnam and who could prove that their lives would be in danger if Saigon fell. He also cabled Hanoi and the PRG urging "magnanimity to past opponents". On 22 April Whitlam announced in Parliament that certain Vietnamese would be admitted to Australia "for temporary residence". Only around 600 were expected to qualify; also to be admitted were a small number of skilled migrants. The Opposition condemned the response as inadequate and inhumane. Vietnamese students in Australia protested outside Parliament House that extended families were not allowed asylum. In Saigon the beleaguered [Australian Ambassador] Price believed that the Government was prepared to abandon men and women to cruel fates so as not to offend Hanoi.

. . . The Embassy began to evacuate its staff on 23 April; those left were besieged by desperate Vietnamese seeking asylum and inundated with requests from Australia to bring out individual refugees. For the next two days Price and his staff worked around the clock, achieving what they could for the strictly limited number who met the Government's criteria. . . . He [Price] was driven to the airport by a Vietnamese who had worked for the Embassy for many years, the last ten as its senior driver, but who was now to be left behind. The embassy accountant, also abandoned, was reported to have said: "It is shameful and Australia's name will never be forgotten because of it". In the last few days before the Embassy was closed 3667 adult Vietnamese had applied to come to Australia; 342 received approval, and a mere 76 escaped.

. . . the closing of the Australian Embassy in Saigon marked the end of another unsuccessful military campaign, but one that generated a widespread sense of shame and dishonour. [Leader of the Opposition Malcolm] Fraser called the Government's actions despicable. "Australia has turned its back", he said,

> on the many thousands of Vietnamese who supported the cause of democracy and then rejected the handful of people who worked for the Australian Government itself. One can only hope that the North Vietnamese troops who are now overrunning the country show more compassion than the Whitlam Government.

The Government blamed the restrictions placed by the RVN authorities and claimed that Australia had taken more refugees than any other nation excepting the United States, but gained little support. Journalists ranging from the experienced Denis Warner, one of the last Australian journalists to leave Saigon, to Mungo MacCallum of the radical *Nation Review* all saw the circumstances as discreditable. MacCallum quoted a Labor man as saying that Australia lied its way into Vietnam and was now lying its way out.

The Government's reputation was further damaged by the leaking of the cables to Hanoi and Saigon of 2 April. . . . On 29 April the *Age* published the cables . . . On the following day, 30 April, an Australian television journalist, Neil Davis, filmed the last act of the war, as a North Vietnamese tank crashed through the gates of the presidential palace in Saigon. In this context, Whitlam's misleading statement appeared not only dishonest but unforgivably callous towards the anti-communist Vietnamese and unduly partial towards the communist victors. On 30 April the *Sydney Morning Herald*, in a long and prominent editorial, called the cables affair "the gravest political scandal since Federation" and concluded that "A Government which cannot be trusted, which abuses its power and its command of secrecy, forfeits its right to govern. It should be brought down". . . .

. . . On becoming Leader of the Opposition, Fraser had threatened to use the conservative coalition's majority in the Senate to bring down the Government only if it conducted its business in a "reprehensible" manner. For Fraser, as for the writer of the *Sydney Morning Herald* editorial, Whitlam's reaction to the collapse of Saigon and the plight of refugees was sufficiently reprehensible to begin the process of bringing down the Government. Moreover, and more seriously, the Government faced Fraser's challenges just as Australia's long economic boom was ending. This was partly an outcome of the Vietnam War. By official calculations the Menzies, Holt, Gorton and McMahon Governments had spent about $247 million on the Vietnam commitment, not including $6 million in military assistance. The cost of maintaining the armed forces that served in Vietnam amounted to another $218 million. These sums were minuscule compared with military expenditure during the two world wars and were absorbed with little effect on the Australian economy. The same could not be said for the United States. Washington's vast military effort in Vietnam was immensely costly, but the Johnson administration had tried to fund it without raising taxes. The inevitable result was inflation and a huge budgetary deficit. As the American economy began to falter in the early 1970s, so did those of other nations that depended on American investment and trade, including Australia. As businesses and workers tried to combat the effects of inflation, wages and prices spiralled ever higher. When Arab oil producers raised the cost of petroleum to unprecedented levels, the damage was enormous. By late 1975, the halcyon days of full employment and low inflation were over.

No democratic government could escape the wrath of an electorate that felt its living standards declining. In November, after catastrophic errors by the Government and vitriolic attacks by the Opposition, the Governor-General removed Whitlam from office and ensured an election in which Labor was badly beaten. Although a major contributor to its own misfortune, the Labor Party could also claim, by a bitter irony, to be in part a victim of the war that it had opposed for a decade.

Conclusions

The principal argument raised by the defenders of the [Vietnam] commitment was one foreshadowed at least as early as 1966 in Gerald Stone's book *War Without Honour*— that it gave time for the other countries of Southeast Asia to consolidate their political and economic structures before coping with the impact of a communist victory in the region. Both at the time and subsequently, Lee Kuan Yew and his Singaporean colleagues were outspoken advocates of this view. Other Southeast Asian leaders were more discreet but no less grateful that they had not passed through what Lee had called the "mincing machine" that would have resulted if the Vietnamese communists had been victorious in 1965 instead of 1975. Of particular interest to Australians was the suggestion that the anti-communist generals in Indonesia might not have had the self-confidence to resist the attempted communist takeover in 1965, if Saigon had already fallen. No objective test of this thesis could be advanced, but it at least appeared plausible. Some Australians maintained that their Government was wise to maintain its support for the United States, even in this most costly and painful of commitments for their great and powerful friend. . . .

The criticisms went beyond the tactics and methods to the fundamental aims of the Western intervention in Vietnam. Critics pointed to the fallacy of supposing that there had been a threat of communist expansionism in Southeast Asia, comparable with that demonstrated by Stalin and his allies in eastern Europe in the late 1940s. Asia was different, as indicated by the fact that when European, Moscow-centered communism collapsed in the late 1980s, Asian communism survived, in China and North Korea as well as in Vietnam. Ho Chi Minh, many asserted, should have been seen as the voice of Vietnamese nationalism rather than as an instrument of international communism. The post-1975 rivalries between communist regimes in East and Southeast Asia, which sometimes erupted into open warfare, exposed the myth of a monolithic communist bloc in which the Vietnamese in Hanoi were seen as the puppets of Beijing. In any case, the fate of South Vietnam was shown to have little bearing on the national security of Australia (and even less on that of the United States). Communists took power in Laos and Cambodia at the same time as in South Vietnam, but non-communist governments in the rest of Southeast Asia stood firm. The domino theory was therefore ridiculed, especially the more extreme versions that had been put forward in 1965 . . .

So, after three decades of debate over Australia's involvement in the Vietnam War, the middle ground of Australian opinion was that it had been a mistake; while one minority contended that it had been worse, an immoral aggression; and another minority argued that the commitment had been worthwhile, because of its contribution to regional stability.

Discussion Questions: SEATO Allies "Down Under"

1. How did changes in global and regional affairs affect the Nixon Administration's perceptions of Vietnam?

2. Was it in the best interests of Australia to be involved in the Vietnam War? What is opinion there today on the subject?

3. Why did Australia eventually decide to withdraw forces? What problems did it face for the withdrawal?

4. From December 18 to December 29, 1972 President Nixon ordered the massive bombing of targets in the Hanoi-Haiphong area. Did this bombing succeed? What were consequences of this decision?

5. What is your view of the Whitlam Government during the Fall of Saigon?

6. What primary sources might you use to learn more about perspectives of Australia, New Zealand, or another British Commonwealth nation on some episode of the Vietnam War during the Nixon-Ford Years?

IV. Epilogue: The 20th and 25th Anniversaries of the Fall of Saigon

The Bangkok Post, 1995, 2000*

Editorial, April 28, 1995, p. 4
"Southeast Asia joins hands in the aftermath of a war"

Like many other events in today's fast changing world, the Vietnam war seems like a distant event. The business of looking to the future has been handled remarkably well, in many ways. Vietnam was an extremely bitter war, which saw Thailand involved in many ways. This country provided refuge to the revolutionary Ho Chi Minh, sent troops to fight against the communists in the late 1960s, and suffered tension and harm from the Hanoi-inspired conflict in Cambodia during the 1980s. It is notable how much of this historical baggage has been put behind in such a short time.

In Vietnam and elsewhere, the official end of the American war will be celebrated on Sunday [April 30]. Participating in the various formal and informal events will be a wide range of Vietnamese and foreigners who only recently were at each other's throats. The American flag flies from dozens of office buildings and shops. Every nation which sent troops to fight the current government is represented in Vietnam by businessmen, tourists, diplomats, aid workers and more. Battlefields now are tourist attractions. . . .

There have been few wars in history as widely debated as the Vietnam war. There was division and debate in Thailand throughout the conflict. We played host to 50,000 American forces, and allowed them the use of our territory as air, naval and army bases. Thai troops fought in Vietnam and in Laos against the communists. For this support of our friends and principles, Thailand was labelled and criticised. Many of these critics claimed that when Thailand asked the Americans to withdraw their forces in 1976 that our country could not survive, let alone prosper.

The critics were wrong. History will long debate whether Thailand and its non-communist neighbours took the correct course through the Vietnam War, and whether its prosperity was because of the long conflict, or in spite of it. Certainly "the dominoes," in the analogy of former U.S. President Dwight Eisenhower, did not topple. But there are many who argue that the Vietnam conflict gave the Southeast Asian countries outside Indochina a chance to become stable. Thai movement towards democracy has been lurching, rather than steady. . . .

The official—if not the actual—end of the Vietnam War will be marked on Sunday. It is encouraging the anniversary will be remembered with little disagreement. Certainly, the chances of war have receded. In a world where wars are being fought over issues a century old or more, this is a matter of note. In less than a generation, we have moved from a fighting war to a spirit of accord. This seems like it is worthy of a day of celebration.

***Bangkok Post,* May 2, 1995, Inside Indochina section, p. 1**
"Quest to rebuild mutual trust"
Nassara Sawatsawang and Bhanravee Tansubhapol

Thailand's role in the Vietnam War remains a source of debate because of its impact on the kingdom's economy, national security, culture and the crucial question of trust between Thailand and its Indochinese neighbours.

The fear of being the next "domino" to fall under communism, as nationalist guerrillas in Laos and Vietnam waged independence wars, drove Thailand into the war.

Privy Councillor Gen Pichitr Kullavanijaya, one of those involved in the war, told *Inside Indochina* had it not been for the Thai government's decision to send troops to Vietnam, Thailand could not have succeeded in suppressing its own communist insurgency.

"Fighting outside the country was better so we could avoid damage to the country, as well as to people's morale," he said.

The communist threat is where U.S. policy and Thailand's security interests converged. Thailand's decision to take an active part in the war was also motivated by two other factors: the need to rehabilitate the Thai army that suffered during World War II and the need for the military dictatorship of Field Marshal Sarit Thanarat to sustain its rule through a superpower alliance, according to analysts.

Under those circumstances, Thailand in 1954 joined the Southeast Asia Treaty Organisation (SEATO) set up by the U.S. with a view to countering communism in Southeast Asia. SEATO's associate members were the United States, Australia, New Zealand, Britain, France, Thailand, the Philippines and Pakistan.

Eight years later, Thailand and the U.S. signed what was known as the Rusk-Thanat agreement which prescribed mutual assistance in the event of communist attack.

The pact was not activated until 1967 when Thailand first sent troops of the Queen's Cobra task force to help the U.S. fight northern communists in South Vietnam.

The Thai troops were stationed at Nui Dat, the area between Vung Tau and Nha Be, while the headquarters, led by task force commander Maj-Gen Yos Dhepahasdin, was in Saigon to facilitate communications with the U.S. command.

Thai soldiers arrived in Vietnam continuously during 1967–71. The 2,000 troop Queen's Cobra task force evolved into the "Black Panther" division numbering 6,000.

Gen Pichitr, who served as an administration assistant in division three of the Queen's Cobra task force, recalled that it was an eye-opening experience in learning new know-how and combat strategies.

"The Thai troops in Vietnam learned the use of helicopters in various situations and to make strategic plans. It was useful for subsequent suppression of communist insurgency in Thailand," he said.

The Thai-U.S. alliance for the Vietnam War served the Thai national interest at that time and the U.S. interest was met in terms of stationing its bases and troops in Thailand.

Among air and naval bases used during the war, the famous U-Tapao air base at Sattahip, Chon Buri province, was where B52 fighter-bombers left to bomb Vietnam. Other facilities to support the U.S. combat operations in Vietnam were in the northeastern provinces of Nakhon Ratchasima, Ubon Ratchathani and Udon Thani as well as Taklee airport for logistics operations in the north-central province of Nakhon Sawan.

The war stimulated the Thai economy, especially in the Northeast. Various forms of U.S. aid valued around U.S. $1.059 billion, or an annual average flow of $151.3 million reached Thailand, according to "A Study of American Multilateral and Bilateral Assistance to Northeast Thailand since the 1950s", conducted by Prachoom Chomchai, former assistant executive agent of the Mekong Committee.

The U.S. was a key donor to the now-defunct committee grouping Laos, Vietnam, Cambodia and Thailand.

Through its aid agency USAID, the U.S. helped construct airfields and naval facilities, as well as many roads in the Northeast to enable mobility of its Vietnam operations.

Among the major road links were the Prachin Buri-Kabin Buri route that was linked to the construction of U-Tapao air base, as well as the Korat-Lomsak-Pitsanulok strategic road network. Airstrips supporting U.S. operations in Vietnam were built at Khon Kaen's Nam Phong Dam, Nakhon Ratchasima, Nakhon Phnom, Udon Thani, Nakhon Sawan and Ubon Ratchathani.

The U.S. aid to Thailand during the war was not alone in boosting the northeastern economy, according to academic Theera Nuchpiem of Silpakorn University. After the end of the war in 1975, the Thai government had its own reason to allocate resources to its own poorest region for domestic strategic reasons.

"The Communist Party of Thailand's infiltration in the Northeast was strong. It was therefore essential for the government to enforce its presence in the area," Theera said.

Government efforts to assert its presence and develop the Northeast spawned activities like the accelerated rural development and community development schemes in provinces along the Mekong River. The government built schools and hospitals, sent mobile development units to offer medical treatment and distributed anti-communist propaganda leaflets. Development programmes started for strategic reasons remain in use.

Except for the Nakhon Sawan air base, other airports built during the war have been converted to commercial use, such as those in Nakhon Ratchasima, Udon Thani and Ubon Ratchathani.

U-Tapao air base, with permanent fixtures and standard runways upgraded since the war, is slated to become a heavy maintenance centre to service aircraft and to be an air cargo transport hub planned as part of Thailand's ambitious Global Transpark.

While the Thai government took advantage of the economic development, the advent of the war left some unpalatable marks socially for Thailand.

The simple way of life in rural areas has changed since that time because of the influx of American dollars, according to former student activist Wuthipong Lakkham.

Apart from the boom in house and car rental services, the *mia chao* or wife-for-hire, an arrangement under which some American servicemen kept commercial sex workers as temporary companions, made its appearance.

"It was a period of a sharp decline of morality in Thai society," Wuthipong said.

The number of criminals rose and many people got into the illegal trade in weapons.

"You could just put weapons in your bags and transport them across provinces unsuspected," he said.

Gen Pichitr agrees, adding that some Thai soldiers turned themselves into gunmen because of the temptation of money.

Perhaps another thing Thailand lost during the war that it is trying hard to regain is the trust of neighbouring countries.

With the end of the war, Thailand shifted its policy into befriending its neighbours.

Under the Seni Pramoj government, then Foreign Minster Pichai Rattakul was sent to Vietnam and Laos to restore diplomatic ties in August 1976. Relations with Vietnam, in particular, bounced back to normal faster than most expected because Vietnam wanted to have friends after the end of the war, Dr. Theera said.

Confirming the speed of recovery in Thai-Vietnamese relations, former Thai ambassador to South Vietnam Col Pattana Payakaniti confirmed Hanoi had no qualms about the return of former second secretary of the Thai Embassy in Saigon Rangsan Phaholyothin to serve as the Thai ambassador to Vietnam in Hanoi.

However, distrust still runs deep between Thailand and Vietnam.

Throughout the Cold War that persisted after 1975, Thailand remained wary of communist Laos and Vietnam.

Col Pattana said he once proposed to form a Thailand-Vietnam

Friendship Association to promote culture, education and sports exchanges during the time of Gen Chatichai Choonhavan's administration. But the idea was rejected by both Gen Chatichai and the National Security Council.

Despite the top-level pledge of cementing ties, leaving the past behind and looking ahead, Thailand and Vietnam still have to exercise more efforts to implement that ideal.

***Bangkok Post,* May 2, 1995, Inside Indochina section, p. 2**
"Report"
Bhanravee Tansubhapol and Nussara Sawatsawang

Gen Pichitr Kullavanijaya, former administration assistant of Division 3, the Queen's Cobra Task Force:

"From a military point of view, our Vietnam experiences gave us lessons about strategic planning and handling of massive armaments and shells in a way unprecedented in our country.

"That was useful for us at the subsequent stage when he devised tactics to fight communist insurgency in our country. Learning from the combat experiences in the Vietnam War, we managed to both contain the communist insurgency in the country and stop Thailand from being the next to fall in the 'domino theory'.

"Having said that, however, I think we failed in the sense that we only helped fight the communists in Vietnam, but not against poverty there. It was a waste to pour money into the corrupt Saigon government and not to help the poor people.

"If the people are not poor, how can they become communists? Even now, communism can make a comeback in the event of a very wide wealth gap. And what we can do to fill this gap is education."

Dr Theera Nuchpiam, vice-president for international affairs, Silpakorn University:

"It is understandable within the context of the communism threat at that time for Thailand to enter the Vietnam War. But when time passed, many questions surfaced, such as where was our national interest? What were we doing? Why did we interfere in Vietnamese affairs? None of these could be answered.

"The upshot for Thailand in this case is neither victory nor defeat. The Thai leadership thought they were right to ally with the United States to fight the communists, in addition to gaining a large amount of (U.S. dollar) assistance and some personal benefits.

"Yet what I felt was that the Thais at that time were not as panic-stricken as their leaders. The government's public campaign only featured street billboards carrying big pictures of a man identified as communist.

"On the contrary, I think Thai people were sympathetic with the Vietnamese people's sufferings during French colonial rule."

Col Pattana Payakniti, Thai ambassador to the Republic of Vietnam 1971–73:

"There were high risks at that time because the Thai embassy was one of 30 embassies in Saigon being targeted for attacks by the Viet Cong. But it was not attacked.

When I was there, only about 30 Thai soldiers remained. U.S. fighter-bombers and Viet Cong missiles were still active and so many bomb-equipped helicopters were flying all over the city.

"I was very scared. Apart from a gun under my pillow, I always carried a submachinegun and a hand grenade just in case any Viet Cong stormed my bedroom.

"My position as a soldier was useful for communication with the American commander and, whenever something happened, I could contact the Supreme Command Headquarters directly.

"The U.S., I think, lost the war in Vietnam not because of its military weakness, but for its domestic political reasons."

Wongse Polnikorn, a member of the World War II Free Thai Movement, permanent secretary of the Foreign Ministry during 1976–77 and Nong Khai MP in 1981 and 1986:

"It's the Pridi Bhanomyong government which initiated the policy of supporting our neighbouring countries' independence struggle. We, members of the Free Thai Movement, politicians and northeastern MPs supplied those independent fighters with arms and other support. So Thailand, Laos and Vietnam were very close.

"I disagreed totally with the policy of the military regime (which ousted the Pridi government) to interfere and send troops to Vietnam because what (the northern Vietnamese) fought for was reasonable and correct."

"It was wrong for Thailand to take part in the Vietnam War from both the humanitarian and good-neighborliness points of view. It's not fair for the Thai government to use its own yardstick to identify people as 'communists' anywhere.

"As a result of the Vietnam War, the Thai government came up with a brutal policy to suppress the communist insurgency. The thrust of it was 'the three alls' namely, all-out weeding; burn all and kill all. That gave the licence for some officials to charge and kill innocent people.

"I really don't care if we had not taken part in the war. Thais should have had the right to choose whether we would join the war.

"Vietnam was always at war and poor; and that's because it had no other choice or opportunities. But now we can see lots of foreign investment and potential there. So probably being a socialist country is not always 'bad'."

***Bangkok Post,* April 27, 2000, p. 12**
"Saigon: after the fall"
Alexander Casella

Saigon, April 30, 1975, 11:30 am. The red and blue flag of the national Liberation Front, with at its centre the golden star of the Vietnamese Communist party is raised over the Presidential Palace.

After 21 years of a tottering existence, the Republic of Vietnam collapsed like a house of cards. For the ageing leaders of Hanoi's Politburo, a dream had come true. Ho Chi Minh is dead but his successors have remained true to his last will: To make Vietnam "Free, Independent. Unified and Socialist."

But the dream endures. For the leaders in Hanoi, the end of the war does not mean the end of the struggle. Within their grand design they see their struggle not as an isolated event but as part of the world-wide confrontation between the socialist bloc and the forces of imperialism.

Vietnam, in their eyes, is the "vanguard of the socialist revolution in Southeast Asia."

The next step will be the consolidation of the three Indo-Chinese states in a "special relation." The reconstruction of Vietnam will follow, with the emphasis on total collectivisation, industrialisation on the Stalinist model and the reorganisation of the country into massive agro-industrial units. . . .

April 30, 2000.
A quarter of a century has passed. The Soviet Union has collapsed. The "world revolution" is part of history and the model is no longer Lenin but Lee Kwan Yew [Prime Minister of Singapore]. Conversely, Vietnam's communist party is still in power. It has decollectivised land ownership, is in the process of privatising trade and industry and has become a full member of Asean [Association of Southeast Asian Nations, formed to cooperate to promote the growth and stability of the region; Vietnam was admitted in 1995]. After having won the war, it is now, twenty-five years later, slowly winning the peace. Since its birth, some three thousand years ago, Vietnam can be defined by one word: resistance. Resistance against the forces of nature. The Red River delta, the cradle of the Vietnamese nation is some nine-to-twelve feet below the level of the river. It took one thousand years to build the intricate network of dikes that protect the rice fields that nurture the community. Their upkeep is a constant struggle and the threats of flood and typhoon are ever present. Resistance against the overwhelming presence of China. A presence so massive in its cultural impact that it could not be resisted otherwise than through an unending process in which war alternated with accommodation.

It is through this process that the Vietnamese acquired the uncanny ability to assimilate foreign cultural inputs while retaining a passionate national identity. . . .

In another environment, America's endeavour [during the Vietnam War] might have succeeded. But Vietnam was too ancient, too complex, too devious, too tangled, too resilient.

Ultimately, America only succeeded in destroying the dignity of those it sought to assist.

The communist ethic, however flawed its ideology, had bridged the gap between tradition and revolution, between respect for a hierarchal social order and the aspirations of a peasant society to greater social justice and national fulfilment.

Likewise, their leaders were credible.

Many were village scholars, people of simple origin but highly educated, or self educated.

On the ground, the soldiers on both sides were the same; eighteen year old farm boys.

On one side they had officers who shared their hardships, they were fighting foreigners or their associates so as to reunify their ancestral land as per the wishes of their benign and revered uncle Ho.

On the other side, there was disorder, corruption and confusion;

keeping Thieu in power was not what the average Vietnamese was ready to die for. Ideology was never part of the picture. Whatever the motivation of his leaders, the average Viet Cong or North Vietnamese soldier had little use for dialectical materialism.

Fighting foreigners was however closer to his heart and mind.

Thus, ultimately, all the Communists had to do was to wait for the Americans to leave. When the hour of reckoning came, in the Spring of 1975, two years after the Americans had pulled out their last troops, the Republic of Vietnam had the world's fourth largest army. But numbers proved irrelevant. It did not have the Mandate of Heaven.

The Communist offensive started on March 10, where it was the least expected, at Ban Me Thuot.

Forty-eight hours later the city had fallen, precipitating a major rout from the Central highlands.

On March 20 Thieu announced on the radio that the enemy had been defeated. Eleven days later Danang, the most heavily defended city of South Vietnam fell when guerrillas drove to the center of town announcing that the city had been liberated.

By then, practically all the officers had fled and most of the soldiers were in their underwear, having thrown away their uniforms. With the fall of Danang it became obvious to all, except the U.S. embassy in Saigon that the game was over. The price of the war for Vietnam was: three million casualties, 40 years of isolation, a North reduced to rubble and a South with a fractured social thermostat.

It was a mortgage that the regime was to pay for years. Nothing prepared the Communists for their 1975 victory.

For 30 years [1945–1975] their one priority was winning the war. With the exception of a botched land reform in 1956 the Communist Party had no experience in running a peace-time economy.

It was only when the country's economy came close to collapsing that the leadership realized that the Marxist dogmas of the [nineteen] twentys did not provide the answers to the challenges of the twenty first century and that ideology was no substitute for geopolitical realities. The collapse of the Soviet Union, brought about the third liberation of Vietnam; the road towards "Renovation" on which Vietnam embarked in 1985 officially brought the country back from the brink of collectivisation.

Substantially, however, it was far more than just another economic option. It was Vietnam finally confronting its own reality without reference to a "Model." The end result will no doubt be a far cry from what Vietnam's revolutionary fathers had originally envisaged.

Discussion Questions: Epilogue

1. What were the War's economic and social effects on Thailand?

2. Suggest outcomes had Thailand not entered the Vietnam War.

3. In *The Bangkok Post* articles, May 2, 1995, the last interviewee (Wongse Polnikorn) said that what the North Vietnamese "fought for was reasonable and correct." Was it? What did the Government of North Vietnam fight for?

4. How did Vietnam in 2000 differ from Vietnam in 1975?

5. Which view of Thailand in the Vietnam War struck you most, and why?

6. Was the Vietnam War a mistake, necessary (to give Southeast Asian countries time), or morally unjust?

Suggestion for Undergraduate Research

Propose a topic for a research paper, based on primary sources, about a non-American perspective on the Vietnam War

or

Submit a research proposal with an engaged (service) learning component—for example, *re* refugees or veterans—or a peace and justice studies component—e.g., possible alternatives to war.

*Notes: Works Excerpted

I. A. Robert M. Blackburn, *Mercenaries and Lyndon Johnson's "More Flags": The Hiring of Korean, Filipino and Thai Soldiers in the Vietnam War* (Jefferson, North Carolina and London: McFarland, 1994), pp. 1–5, 7–8, 11, 22–23, 30–32, 48–50, 52–55, 58–59, 61–65, 72–73, 80, 82–84, 88–93, 95, 98–100, 102–115.

B. Robert J. McMahon, *The Cold War on the Periphery: The United States, India, and Pakistan* (New York: Columbia University Press, 1994), pp. 307–308, 318–329, 331–332, 334–335.

II. Caroline Page, *U.S. Official Propaganda during the Vietnam War, 1965–1973: The Limits of Persuasion* (London and New York: Leicester University Press, 1996), pp. 106–110, 112–113, 120–124, 128–133, 135–144, 146–147, 149–150, 154–155, 158–159, 161–162, 165, 174–179.

III. Peter Edwards, *A Nation at War: Australian Politics, Society and Diplomacy during the Vietnam War*, 1965–1975 (St. Leonards, Australia: Allen & Unwin in association with the Australian War Memorial, 1997), pp. 185–195, 198, 201–205, 240–241, 243–246, 262–264, 292, 297, 303–306, 313–318, 321–326, 328–329, 331–332, 335–340, 342–344.

IV. *The Bangkok Post*, 1995, 2000:
[Editorial,] "Southeast Asia Joins Hands in the Aftermath of a War," April 28, 1995, p. 4. Nussara Sawatsawang and Bhanravee Tansubhapol, "Quest to Rebuild Mutual Trust," May 2, 1995, Inside Indochina section, p. 1. Bhanravee Tansubhapol and Nussara Sawatsawang, "Report," May 2, 1995, Inside Indochina section, p. 2. Alexander Casella, "Saigon: After the Fall," April 27, 2000, p. 12.

Index

Note: Some entries that appear throughout the book, such as United States, Vietnam, and Vietnam War, are not listed in the *Index*.